Come to the

Banquet

Nourishing

Our Spiritual

Hunger

Come to the Banquet

Nourishing Our Spiritual Hunger

Donna,
I hope you find
this of some value!
J. Muldoon

TIM MULDOON

SHEED & WARD

Franklin, Wisconsin
Chicago

As an apostolate of the Priests of the Sacred Heart, a Catholic religious congregation, the mission of Sheed & Ward is to publish books of contemporary impact and enduring merit in Catholic Christian thought and action. The books published, however, reflect the opinions of their authors and are not meant to represent the official position of the Priests of the Sacred Heart.

2002

Sheed & Ward
7373 South Lovers Lane Road
Franklin, Wisconsin 53132
1-800-266-5564

Printed in the United States of America

Cover and interior design by Robin Booth
Cover photo: Copyright © DigitalVision/PictureQuest
Author photo by Fred Kipp of Kipp Photography in Indiana, PA

Library of Congress Cataloging-in-Publication Data
Muldoon, Tim
    Come to the Banquet : nourishing our spiritual hunger / Tim Muldoon.
        p.cm.
    Includes bibliographical references.
    ISBN 1-58051-119-8 (pbk.)
      1. Christian life. 2. Christianity. I. Title.

BV4501.3 .M83 2002
248.4—dc21
                                        2002017741

Dedication

· · ·

To the memory of my cousin,
John Kevin O'Connor

TABLE OF CONTENTS

ACKNOWLEDGMENTS

I wish to thank those whose encouragement, support, shared stories, and enthusiasm helped make this book a reality. It arose out of my encounter with students at the Newman Centers at Emory University and Indiana University of Pennsylvania, as well as with the many students who have passed through my classes at Duquesne University, Seton Hill College, and especially Mount Aloysius College.

Of particular note are those Mount Aloysius students who, in the "Seminar in Theology," read and gave comments on the manuscript. Thanks also to Rev. Jerome Machar, O.C.S.O., of the Abbey of the Genesee who gave helpful feedback on an earlier version; to Edward Schmidt, S.J., whose enthusiasm for the book was of great help; and to my friends Joanne Wakim and Dave Sloan whose encouragement was valuable to me. Finally, thanks to my editors, Jeremy Langford and Kass Dotterweich, for their insightful suggestions.

In a different vein, I wish to acknowledge the ways that my wife, Suzanne, and daughter, Grace, have buoyed me through the process of writing. In the comfort of my family I have been sustained and challenged, and I am grateful.

Christian Spirituality
in the New Millennium

Young people, myself included, like to think of ourselves as free thinking, able to choose for ourselves, able to distinguish what's new or old, hip or out of date. We don't like the idea of following like sheep and accepting blindly whatever our culture tells us is the right thing at the moment. We like individuality and uniqueness. But if you're like me, you observe sometimes that this quest for uniqueness means having to be unique in the same ways as your friends. You dress, speak, act differently than your parents, but in order to do this you dress, speak, and act exactly like your friends. I walk onto the campus where I teach looking legitimately different from my students—they wear the latest clothes, I wear a tie. I'm the individual, the unique one, but I'm treated differently. People seem to accept only so much uniqueness. Off campus, I drive around town dressed like the students, and I blend right in. At least being like everyone else is comfortable.

The easy part of acting like people around us is that we don't have to constantly face the reality of being different. It can be hard sometimes. But at different times of my life, I have sought to distance myself from the common way of doing things because I thought I owed it to myself. I don't want other people making choices for me; I want to be the one who determines the course of my life.

Some choices, of course, are made for us. I didn't choose where to be born, for example, what language to speak, or my own name. I'm here whether I like it or not. What's more, my culture affects the choices I make: I have certain expectations about things like school, money, friends, job choices, and other things because I live in the

United States rather than somewhere like Japan or Brazil. So I try to be aware of the ways that, in a sense, my choices are made for me.

Our purpose here is to focus on our choice about religion. Too often we make our choices based more on what the culture expects, rather than thinking through for ourselves what any given choice means for us personally. In other words, our own thinking about religion and spirituality can give us more freedom to make a good choice for ourselves. Religion is about commitment—the very word comes from the Latin word which means "to bind." If we understand faith as the way we respond to God in our lives, religion is the way we decide to commit ourselves to act on faith. But unless we seriously think about it, our decisions will be made for us, and we will lose an important way of deciding what kind of people we can be.

A simple illustration will help show what I mean. In the past, adult children followed their parents' religious decisions; Jewish traditions, for example, were passed from one generation to the next. The same with Catholic traditions. Today, however, many adult children are not satisfied with blindly agreeing to whatever their parents say; they want to take control of their beliefs and practices. We tend to think that those who make these decisions are thinking more seriously about their religion, as opposed to those who appear simply to be following Mom's and Dad's rules without really thinking about it.

The picture, however, is much more complex. There are those people, for example, who are more lazy than thoughtful; they simply do not practice religion because they consider it boring. Yet, is this any better than the child who mindlessly chooses to continue to practice his or her parents' tradition? Is the one who stops going to church because it's boring making a thoughtful decision about his or her life? I would argue that it's the opposite: perhaps the person is avoiding a decision because in our culture, religion just is not seen as all that important. In other words, it is common *not* to make a decision about religion, because religion is seen as old-fashioned.

This is a problem. If religion is about ultimate things like life and death and God and truth and love and suffering, then not making a thoughtful decision about religion is to take lightly the very essence of life itself. The French philosopher Blaise Pascal said it well: not to make a decision about God is to make a decision—namely, to believe God is irrelevant. Honestly confronting Christian spirituality means confronting one of the most important decisions of our lives—and the more we think about it, the freer our decision can be. A careful and purposeful consideration of Christian spirituality means that we're not just following the crowd; rather, we're making a statement about ourselves.

Why Spirituality?

I choose to practice Christian spirituality not because my parents told me to, or because I'm afraid of going to hell if I don't, or because of my friends, or because of some deep-seated unconscious need unfulfilled from childhood, or any other simple explanation. I choose to practice Christian spirituality because it helps me to negotiate the most meaningful moments of life, and to make sense of the realities of suffering and genuine love. I don't have any syrupy answers or catchphrases that seem to ignore real life. I don't like that old proselytizing Bible thumping "believe or you're going to hell." I'm not a retro-weirdo who still believes we're in the Middle Ages. Rather, I see myself as someone who has been given a gift—and I invite you, in the same way that once upon a time someone invited me, to consider the wisdom of the Christian tradition. And I extend this invitation, believing that while sometimes individual churches can be boring or irrelevant, the Church remains a place where honest people help each other seek God and live good lives, following the example of Jesus.

Because the word *spirituality* is used so often today, it merits some clarification as it is used here. The word comes from the Latin word *spiritus*, which means both "spirit" and "breath," suggesting that the animating feature of human life is breathing. In the Book of Genesis, it is God's Spirit that hovers over the waters at the dawn of creation and is breathed by God into Adam. In the Gospel of John, Jesus breathes his spirit on the disciples, telling them to forgive people's sins and to preach the gospel. We'll address later what texts like these mean for people who live in a postmodern world, but for now, let us consider that Christian "spirituality" refers to the practice of responding to God's presence in the world. This notion finds its clearest expression in a text from the First Letter of Paul to the Corinthians: "[N]o one can say 'Jesus is Lord' except by the Holy Spirit" (12:3). Christian spirituality is the practice, discipline, and dialogue of acknowledging Jesus as Lord through the gift of God's spirit, God's self—and the living of that conviction in everyday life.

In light of the fact that we live in a culture that offers so many ways to approach life other than through the practice of Christian faith, we ask the question, Why spirituality? First of all, *spirituality* is the practice of trying to find meaning in our lives, the attempt to draw from a wisdom that transcends our sometimes meager attempts to answer the hard questions of life. Taking spirituality seriously allows us to examine some basic truths upon which Christian faith is based, thus providing us with some appreciation of what it means for people to claim, "Jesus is Lord." Spirituality is about seeking wisdom, in that it is the constant practice of drawing from a source of meaning that is greater than ourselves. For me, this means that spirituality begins by recognizing that the world is mysterious, and that I alone cannot pretend to have all the answers. It means believing that even when I confront suffering, I can draw strength from faith in a God whose ways I don't always understand, or even agree with. It means appreciating my own limitations in understanding why there is evil, but at the same time retaining that terrible but beautiful gift of hope in spite of myself.

Spirituality, then, is not an attempt to run away from the world or to create some illusion about suffering. On the contrary, spirituality is about having the courage to confront the world as it really is: good and evil, beautiful and ugly, profoundly meaningful and yet sometimes (it seems) completely meaningless. It involves the recognition that human knowledge alone cannot help us answer the most basic questions, like "Why are we here?" or "What are we supposed to do with our lives?" And it is about keeping open that most enigmatic of questions: "Who is God?"

I do not pretend to be the most spiritual person. I must admit that spirituality can be difficult; prayer can be tedious and frustrating. But I continue to believe that like so many parts of our lives, it is the working through these difficult times that make it ultimately more worthwhile. As difficult as it is to talk about, God does manifest a personal Self to people who want to know God. And while I don't think this happens in ways we would like or expect, the effect on people still can be profound. In fact, we tend to "see" God more in reverse: that is, when we look back on our lives and understand that we have changed. In my own life, the clearest example of this is the very fact that I do what I do. Many people don't take their faith as seriously as I do, or choose to work in the academic study of theology—and when I take a step back and think about my life choices, I recognize and marvel at how strange this life is! But I don't think I would be living my life in exactly this way if I didn't believe God was somehow involved.

Spirituality is important because it is about responding *for ourselves* to the big claims about life. Do you want someone else to decide for you who God is? Are you content to let popular feeling convince you about the relevance of religion? Are you sure that God doesn't have a plan for you or that you can learn to live in a way that makes you happier and more at peace with yourself? Spirituality is about wrestling *for ourselves* with these questions, and in so doing, making reliable decisions about the kind of lives we choose to lead.

Spirituality in Generation 2000

I use the term *Generation 2000* to indicate what, for many people, is a formative moment. The new millennium signifies an end and a beginning, an instant in history that makes us consider what the past has given us and what the future holds. For those of us who were born near the end of a century and a millennium, the new millennium is a time of great promise, and the use of the term *Generation 2000* is to indicate something of this promise, in contrast to the terms *Gen X* or *Gen Y,* which to me measure the generation of younger adults according to the standards of older ones.[1] For the purpose of clarity, let us for now accept that Generation 2000 are the children born toward the end of the twentieth century; but let us also suggest that Gen2K (as I will call us) are people who are coming of age in this new millennium. And when I say "coming of age," I want to suggest that this is as much a spiritual endeavor as a biological or sociological reality. *Coming of age* means developing a certain self-awareness, a sense of being an individual, and not merely someone else's child or brother or sister. It involves understanding oneself in relation to other people, recognizing one's gifts and strengths as well as liabilities and weaknesses.

Gen2K is a group of young people who sees in the new millennium a historic moment, a kind of mark to distinguish the old from the new, and who can say for ourselves, "the past is prologue; the present is mine." According to different studies, we are into spirituality but not religion.[2] The songs we listen to, the language we use, the symbols we wear on our clothes and on our skin, testify to this fascination with spirituality. And although our group is diverse, and therefore hard to categorize, I venture to suggest several observations that will serve as points of reference impacting our discussion of spirituality.

Information is at our fingertips. Our generation has immediate access to more information than any other generation in history, a fact that contains both a promise and a caution. T. S. Eliot asked, "Where is the wisdom we have lost in knowledge? Where is the knowledge we have lost in information?" Today, the critical issue is not *how much* knowledge we accumulate but *how well* we use this knowledge. Ultimately, the issue is one of wisdom, that ability to organize knowledge, love, experiences, will, humor, work, and everything else that impacts our ability to live in the world. It is an ability to recognize when our culture is leading us in the wrong direction, and to make choices that may be different from those our peers would make in similar situations. It's a basic question: "How should I live?"

For example, think of a time when you were caught in a traffic jam: cars stopped in front of you as far as you could see, with no hint of how long you would be sitting there. At such times, I wish my car could turn into a helicopter so I could rise above the traffic and see what's going on, maybe even tell others some alternate routes. I wish I had a better perspective, a higher viewpoint, a broader horizon.

Another example that comes to mind is the time some friends and I went hiking in the mountains of Wales. When we decided it was time to head back to our lodgings, we'd not only hiked many miles, but a dense fog had rolled in, seriously distorting our sense of direction. After a moment of panic, I was relieved to see that my friend had a detailed map of the landscape, allowing us to make the return trek without incident.

Both of these metaphors point to the idea of our need for direction. It's easy to stumble through life, but difficult to have a clear sense of where we are going. Things would be different if we had a clearer vision of which way to go. The practice of spirituality can give us that clearer vision. And because religion is not always something our culture tells us is good, we have to be somewhat countercultural even to look into it. But consider again the traffic jam: just because a group of people is doing something doesn't mean that they, as individuals, know where they're going.

Our generation has a lot of knowledge, or at least access to it, but that doesn't mean we have wisdom. We need a way to discern what knowledge is actually going to help us build a better world—we need the wisdom of authentic spirituality.

Experience is important. We live in a postmodern world, which means that we tend to be a little suspicious of large institutions and old claims about authority. We need to figure out things for ourselves, and we don't want others telling us how to live. (Rest assured, I won't be doing any of that.) But here we have a problem: life is way too complex for any of us to figure it out alone. So we need ways of discerning who can help us to choose for ourselves what is important.

We begin by taking into account the notion of tradition. I admit, although tradition sometimes seems out of date, its strength ties us to the wisdom of past ages. It would be arrogant to assume that we will develop wisdom only through attention to what is new, exciting, and unprecedented. Indeed, there is much in the modern world that no culture in history ever dreamed of, but there is also much in the ancient world that our culture has never seriously considered. Human experience is rich, vast, but our understanding of it is narrow, limited. We must rely on sources of wisdom that transcend individual perceptions, limited viewpoints, and prejudiced opinions. We must not rely on ourselves alone.

Human history has seen the rise and fall of many attempts at wisdom—and many have failed because they did not lead people to greater and lasting joy, peace, and love. Those wisdom traditions that have lasted are those which appeal to people again and again, for whatever reason. One such tradition of wisdom is Christianity, one that happens to draw the largest number of adherents in the world. This is not to imply a kind of triumphalism, but rather highlights the fact that its attractiveness has not diminished over two millennia. And although attractiveness is not the best measure of a wisdom tradition, it does mean that as wisdom, it sheds light on the human experience in such a way as to provide the kind of conviction for which people are prepared to give their lives. One will not willingly suffer for one's beliefs without conviction, and conviction will not happen unless the truth of the conviction gives meaning to one's life. I like to think of tradition as a long history of people like me confronting the same basic questions about what it means to be human. And so I value it, because it helps me remember that I am not alone, that perhaps the wisdom of life others have gained can help me with my own life.

We question authority. Today's young adults don't think that everything the Church says is right, and won't believe something just because their parents, the Church, or some other authority figure says so. Part of this attitude is about taking seriously what we see as shortcomings in Christian history. For example, how can we believe in a tradition that produced the Crusades and the Inquisition, and sanctioned banned books, witch hunts, and anti-Semitism? How can we trust a group of people that, in the name of faith, shows hateful attitudes toward others—as in the conflicts between Catholics and Protestants and the discriminating behaviors against homosexuals?

No one, of course, has easy solutions to these questions. Despite the countless Internet sites that claim to wield truth and authority (especially when it comes to religion), it's hard to trust any ideology or belief system that produces "bad" people. Yet, there is such a thing as a legitimate authority or a claim to truth—a reliable authority that helps us make sense of the world and enables us to build a better one.

Indeed, Christians have done terrible things in the name of God; but the fault is on the people, not on the wisdom of Christian spirituality. There are imperfect Christians, just as there are imperfect doctors, but this makes neither Christianity nor medicine inherently wrong. Rather, it simply confirms that a body of wisdom or knowledge can have more to offer than its human proponents demonstrate.

We live in a shrinking world. Today's modern technology and our opportunities for travel and study abroad position Gen2K in a world much smaller than the world of our parents. Unlike any previous generation, we see our planet's diversity of lifestyles and value systems, and appreciate the respect due other people's lifestyles and life choices. If there is one overarching ethical statement that Gen2K can claim, it is this: Don't judge.

Here is the problem, though. Unless we judge, we make no decisions about ourselves or for ourselves. That is not to suggest that we be "judgmental" or have some kind of superior attitude toward others. Rather, because we have to make decisions about what kind of life we're going to live, we have to weigh for ourselves what is going to be most life-giving, and this involves judgment—not judgments *of others*, but judgments *about ourselves.*

Spirituality is a fundamental choice because it helps me look beyond the ways people are different, to pay attention to what we all share: our humanity. In a shrinking world, Christianity does not threaten our ability to relate to people different from us. Rather, it helps us see them as equals in the eyes of God. Christianity gives us the courage to admit to and grieve the errors of the past and to commit to a present and a future that celebrates the entire human family. Today, Christian spirituality can help us appreciate our shared humanity and give expression to the deepest yearnings for meaning that transcend our cultural differences.

We hunger for meaning. Our generation can do more, learn more, travel more, and meet more interesting people than ever before. Yet, even with this wealth of advantage and opportunity, an overriding concern for us is a search for *meaning.* We cannot live without meaning, for it is that which enables us to make sense out of everything else. It is the meaning of life that makes us willing to suffer and even die for what we believe.

This observation, however, serves only to highlight that Christianity is attractive; it does not mean that Christianity is true. Advertising can make a product attractive; but ultimately, the product has to prove itself. If Christianity is truly a tradition of wisdom, then it must not only shed light on the human drama but also it must be based in truth.

Nor does addressing the hunger for meaning through an exploration of Christian faith suggest that other wisdom traditions, especially the other major world religions, have nothing to offer. Clearly, the major religions of the world have served to make human beings more conscious of their place in human society and have given meaning to human living. Indeed, the single greatest task of our generation is to engage in interreligious dialogue, especially in an age when the marketplace of ideas involves religious truths. I am convinced, however, that wisdom demands not only the kind of disinterested pursuit of knowledge which science, and the philosophical study of the world's religions, demands. Instead, I follow Saint Augustine in his paraphrase of a text from the book of Isaiah: "I believe, in order that I might understand." Wisdom is not only a *knowledge of* truth, but a *participation in* truth. The Latin word for wisdom, *sapientia*, is related to the verb *sapere*, to taste. A psalm exhorts us to "taste and see the goodness of the Lord," to devote one's whole self to the understanding of God's work. Wisdom is much more like a family dinner than a scientific experiment, and so if we are to find wisdom we must sit down at the banquet and eat.

Thus in our exploration of the truths of the Christian faith, we presuppose that these truths can and do set people free, and that one can be a faithful Christian without, at the same time, being an opponent of other faiths. With this understanding, we can summarize our hunger for meaning in the question, "Is human life the extent of our existence, or is there something more—heaven, or nirvana, or whatever?" Religion provides a certain safety for people, and while some use this safety to stop thinking altogether, others use it thoughtfully to negotiate the difficulty of their existence. We still need to confront our own lives, and so we hunger for a source of wisdom that will satisfy our hunger for meaning. I believe that the banquet which Christian spirituality offers can fill this hunger.

. . .

This book, then, is for people of Gen2K (or people who want to understand Gen2K) who want to ask questions about what Christian spirituality is and what it has to offer them. It is not only for those who call themselves Christian but also for those who might want to confront the claim that Christianity is a wisdom tradition that can help people negotiate the limit questions—those unknowns that define the boundaries of our understanding.

Chapter one begins with an exploration of our hunger for God and how our doubts and biases can keep us from seeking to know God deeply. Chapter two looks at ways in which prayer can serve as spiritual food, the constant source from which we can draw strength to face life's ordinary challenges. Chapter three focuses on the Bible, asking why it has such importance among Christians and why it is recognized as a source of wisdom. Chapter four turns to Jesus, who called himself "the bread of life" in order to emphasize how God seeks to give us what we need. Finally, chapter five looks forward to the ways that Christian spirituality enables us to create lives that respond to God's love in faith, hope, and love.

I ask everyone who reads this to understand my limitations. While Christianity seeks eternal truths, human beings are limited. I aim to help the reader to understand the foundations of Christian faith, but in so doing I cannot help but use the lens through which I, guided by the tradition of which I am a part, see these foundations. It is my hope that this lens will not cloud the readers' vision, but rather, will allow readers to more clearly see the Subject, the Author of Christian wisdom: the God who always and everywhere loves us first.

For Group Discussion

1. How do you think our culture affects the ways people think about God, religion, or spirituality? What are some of the misconceptions people have about being a person of faith? What is your perception of what it means to be a person of faith?
2. How has your own upbringing affected your image of who God is? Who Jesus is?
3. What is spirituality? What examples of spirituality have you encountered in your everyday life or conversation or reading?
4. What are the important differences between your view of the world and your parents'? Do you agree with the characterizations of "Gen2K" here? Why or why not?

5. How has the Internet affected the way we think about information? What are the positive and negative influences of the worldwide web? How does it impact religion?

6. What should churches be doing today? In your experience, are they doing these things? Why or why not?

7. How do you view the relationship between Christians and people of other faiths? What problems exist? What signs of hope do you see?

8. Do people today hunger for meaning? What evidence would you use to support your thinking?

CHAPTER ONE

Hunger:
The Human Hunger for God

Narcotics cannot still the Tooth
That nibbles at the soul—
—EMILY DICKINSON

He who flees from prayer
flees from all that is good.
—ST. JOHN OF THE CROSS

Shakespeare wrote that the whole world is a stage, and that we are actors in the drama of life. If this is true, then our life dramas are confused muddles of tragedy, comedy, romance, epic, and everything in between. Each person is the main actor in his or her own story but, at the same time, each is in a supporting role in the larger story of human history. Yet, at least in this culture, it is easy to imagine ourselves as the stars of the play: individualistic people wanting freedom and independence. As a result, we suffer from seclusion, alienation, and fear of others (just look at road rage as an example). Although there is much to celebrate in American culture, we suffer from a breakdown in community. We don't reach out to our neighbors, and we live in fear of shootings in the workplace, in schools, in community centers—in our own front yards. In such a context, communication breaks down and we lose touch with the most fundamental mysteries of human living. We become overly concerned with ourselves, and our own narrow world—jobs, relationships, entertainment—become most important because they provide us with fantasies about how to be happier than we are right now. Advertisers certainly know this: every ad is about the next thing that will make our lives ever more perfect.

Kairos and Chronos and Meaning

These sober observations suggest that there is a world very different from the one in which we operate every day, a world that becomes clearer when we cease from the busyness of work and play. Anyone who has had a long break from work, perhaps at a beautiful location, has a sense of this. Time just seems to take on a different meaning; we are able to relax and enjoy what the moment has to offer. The ancient Greeks had two words for time: *chronos* and *kairos*. *Chronos* is the root of our word *chronology*, and refers to the everyday world of the clock. *Kairos* refers to a kind of time apart, a time for God, a time away from time. The concept of *kairos* is a key to a world of meaning, a world governed by wisdom. Our lives are too much *chronos* and too little *kairos*—too much hustle and work and not enough joy and peace—but this need not always be the case. Every now and then we need to shut up, shut down, and stop worrying about everything!

We have all experienced the fluidity of time: the wait in a line that seems to take hours, the evening out with friends that disappears quickly. Our experience of *chronos* is governed by the activity in which we are engaged, whether it's something we like or don't like. Large portions of our days are devoted to habitual activity: work, driving, shopping, eating, and other activities that are part of the "grind," routines that we often think ourselves subjects to rather than masters over. Since habits release us from the trouble of having to think about them (when was the last time you *really* paid attention to brushing your teeth?), they can contribute to the evaporation of *chronos* and the ensuing complaint "I never have enough time." This situation has more to do with us, though, than with the activities we perform. We seem to think that we must be busy, as if busyness were the measure of the truly good person. "How have you been?" "Keeping busy." (Why?)

Not long ago I spent some time at a Trappist monastery. The Trappists are an order of priests and brothers who follow the fifth-century Rule of St. Benedict, praying six times a day (beginning at 2 a.m.)

and working to support the life of the community. For me, that time at the monastery was the ultimate experience of *kairos*. I used no clocks (except for that 1:30 a.m. wake-up call!) and did not worry about what I had to do that day or the next or the next. I very simply and gloriously lived in the moment, reveling in being alive. My days were free and simple: I walked from the guesthouse to the monastery, prayed with the monks, worked in the bread-making factory, ate simple meals in community, read, enjoyed nature, and wrote. That was it! My most exciting moments were brief encounters with deer and a snake. Certainly this isn't the makings of headlines in alumni magazines but, for me, it was a wonderful break. It forced me to focus on some basic questions, Why am I alive? What should I do with my life? Whom do I have to please? In pausing from the hurry of life, I was able to ask why I tend to be in such a hurry. In short, this experience of *kairos* confronted me with deep questions of the *meaning* of my life.

Ultimately, *meaning* is that which gives life to our actions, animates and excites us, and gives us zeal for the future and peace in the present. Life is a search for meaning. It demands awareness and vigilance lest, in some passing moment, meaning is revealed in a way we are too lazy to notice. This maxim applies at all stages of life, since the search for meaning continues as long as a person lives. Meaning is not a thing, an object happened upon and possessed. Rather, it is the unfolding of the mystery of life, the encounter with the most basic questions of human existence. Our desire for meaning is deeply personal because it is a desire to make of ourselves people who are good, true, and beautiful. It is that which has been somewhat clumsily called the "search for self."

I have two observations at this point. First, it is strange that people should have to search for themselves. (Where would they look?) Second, if meaning is what motivates human existence, and if the search for self is how we find meaning, it seems that all people should be busy trying to find themselves. If that is the case, then many don't seem to be trying too hard!

We cannot deny that people often seem to feel lost, confused, hopeless. Our generation, in particular, faces the question of meaning in an acute way. Here in this new millennium, we are no longer governed by the structures of family and civil life, social and religious life in the way earlier generations were; we are not bound to follow the patterns of work and family development our grandparents did. People in earlier generations knew their lives were about supporting the family: taking on the family business or farm, following the path that parents chose for them. Many of us in this generation, however, can create the world in which we live to an unprecedented extent: we can choose how much education to pursue, what city to live in, what to do with our sexuality, where to work. This increase in freedom, though, has come with a price. More options mean more chances for error, and such errors are easy to make. Furthermore, we don't necessarily know *how* to choose in a world that offers so many options yet changes so quickly. I call this problem the "cereal-aisle phenomenon"—that feeling you get in the supermarket when you enter the cereal aisle with no idea how to decide between all those choices!

For example, I hear some of my students lament the career choices they made, having learned that the job prospects have dried up. Many of them are in health-related studies, meaning that their hopes for finding employment depend on factors that are outside their control: insurance, Medicare, public perception. They chose their careers based on the once well-justified belief that they could get good jobs, but when the market changed, so did their optimism. This is an example of how a changing world turns good choices into bad, not because of anything these young people have done, but simply because of the way the world works. I have heard similar comments from people who are, by some standards, successful. They graduated and got good jobs, complete with respect and prestige. With time, however they have become bored. They feel like they are pushed day after day to do mundane things that at one time offered charm and challenge. Now all they can see is the next thirty years of their lives stretching out in front of them until they can retire.

The satisfaction we derive from things outside of ourselves—things like jobs, entertainment, and money—can't last, so perhaps this kind of happiness is the wrong thing to search for. In fact, it's difficult to imagine how people can find anything but temporary meaning in things. Temporary meaning cannot satisfy us if we know that some day it will be gone. We long for permanence—the knowledge that what is most meaningful to us will never go away. This, I think, is a hint of our longing for heaven. It also points to those events in our lives that, in the words of many, bring us closest to heaven, like birth, falling in love, and death. How many people have called birth a miracle? How many speak of love as a taste of heaven? And how often have people expressed their hope for heaven in the face of imminent death? These life experiences bring us closer to what is lasting: our relationships with other human beings. In comparison, money, power, sex, work, travel, beauty, and all the other things we pursue in the world of *chronos* are insufficient. In short, the search for ourselves, the search for meaning, is ultimately a search for that which is common to all conscious human beings: the infinite capacity to love and be loved in return. True, people do not need certain basic parts of their lives to come together, but in the end the most perfect outward life is nothing unless that person can also share it with others. The challenge we all face, then, is learning to balance our basic needs with the deeper desires of our hearts. Seeking this balance means seeking wisdom.

"The Fear of the LORD is the Beginning of Wisdom." (Psalm 111:10)

Questions of faith are unlike other questions; they involve the deepest part of a person, and ultimately can be addressed only by the individual. For example, "Who is God?" Have you ever considered *your* answer to this question instead of some answer you've been taught? It is easy to assume that other people "out there" are responsible for our faith. Surely there are priests, nuns, ministers, or rabbis who are supposed to clear up issues of religion, right? This attitude, however, suggests that issues of faith are like issues of science—determined by experts and then passed on to the rest of us, like the doctrines on gravity or relativity. The experts figure it out, then we believe it.

Fortunately, our generation has been suspicious of traditional sources of religious authority, perhaps without knowing why but nonetheless sensing that reality is far more complex than some religious leaders would have us believe. There is, then, both a need for authority and a suspicion about authority, leaving many caught in the gap between real faith and real unbelief.

Unfortunately, the attitude toward religion of many people in our generation is apathy: they neither believe nor disbelieve strongly. For these people, questions of faith in general assume a kind of nonimportance. This is not to say that there are no people of faith in this generation. Clearly there are. But at the level of ordinary conversation, questions of religion don't often come up. Furthermore, religious faith is commonly seen as a private matter: "You have the right to believe what you want, but you may not force it on others." As a result, many people never have a chance to explore the most basic questions about God's relationship to human living. Rather, they make their judgments about religion based on things they learned as children, and never even give themselves the chance to develop a more adult faith. Can we really make good choices about religion if we stopped thinking about it in eighth grade? Our hunger for wisdom demands that we take seriously the question of God, and not simply think that it will take care of itself.

Granted, we cannot figure out God. But facing the mystery of God calls for the guidance of authentic religious authorities, those who can help us understand how people of earlier times sought to understand this mystery. Yet, who is "authentic"? There are plenty of people who claim to know something about religion (just try entering "religion" into your favorite search engine and watch what you get!) but who, in reality, are just full of themselves. Unfortunately, there is no easy way to distinguish the good from the bad in a single look, but there is a reliable guideline: an authentic religious authority is a person or group that helps us to interpret our own experience and understand our own lives in relation to the mystery of God. This person or group must have the weight of tradition, meaning that there is a long line of people who have asked the same questions about God. At the same time, this weight of tradition should not be so heavy that it stifles all that is new. Rather, real authority is about balancing tradition and novelty—it is the ability to bring the wisdom of the past to bear on the problems of the present. Authentic religious authorities call us to consider the richness of what has unfolded in the course of human history. They are like the people who call us to the banquet table; but unless we respond to their calling, we will never partake of the food. Ultimately, of course, it is the individual person who decides to eat or not eat—this is why spirituality is, at its most basic level, a matter of responding to the invitation of God. Religious authorities may help, but they can do nothing unless the believer seeks the wisdom of God. Faith demands effort.

Psalm 111:10 is part of a song of praise to God, written sometime between the fifth and fourth centuries B.C.E. The phrase "fear of the Lord" refers to the activity of the human being rendering praise, thanksgiving, and worship to God. Religion in the ancient world centered on the practice of ritual: one performed certain rites and ceremonies as a response to the various ways God acted in one's life and in the life of the community. Today, such an understanding can help us appreciate why wisdom is not merely some kind of magical way of thinking, but rather a discipline of life, a way of acting for oneself and others.

Wisdom demands action, because God is not visible in the same way that physical objects and other people are visible. Human beings act in a visible world; our actions take place in this physical and finite space. If we are to seek God, then, we must have the capacity to discern our nonphysical God in a physical world. We must learn to see in a new way and appreciate why people who have experienced the loving presence of God use metaphors and colorful language to describe a God who is ultimately not describable. We must learn why different cultures have expressed their understanding of God in ways we no longer use, and therefore understand today only partly. (For example, why is God described in the Bible as a "rock," or as having "eagle's wings"?) We must seek to understand why those who believe in the same God behave very differently and do things we wouldn't. (Why did some Christians of the past become hermits in the desert? Why did others become missionaries?) Finally, we must learn to distinguish holy things from unholy things.

Perhaps most importantly, we must learn to be good people, to do good things. Wisdom is not only a way of thinking and understanding but also a method of acting and responding to others. It is a way of understanding one's life, a life that continues to be expressed in day-to-day actions and the choices that direct those actions. It is a harmony of being and doing, such that the person I understand myself to be is the same person I present to the world.

Fear of the Lord is the beginning of wisdom if we understand "fear" in the sense of reverence or respect (i.e., not like the horror movie variety). It involves taking seriously the claim that God moves in human affairs not as a distant creator or disinterested spectator, but as the co-author of our own life stories, intimately involved in every turn of the plot. It means coming to the understanding of God's will as that which we choose when we are most free. To fear God, to be in awe and wonder at the work of God, is to begin to understand why everything depends on how we respond to this claim, to understand that the very unfolding of our own lives is a testament to the work of God, from the most mundane daily work to the life decisions that affect our future. The story of God's work is the story of our lives.

This is the beginning of wisdom—but only the beginning. We must also understand that the extent of God's work is much greater than this. *Salvation history* is the term often used to describe the unfolding story of God in human history, and it refers to the truth that God has self-revealed in many ways to many people in many cultures—and continues to self-reveal today. The development of the community of faith is the result of this drama. To understand ourselves as players, not merely spectators, in this drama draws us to understand our fellow actors: Abraham and Sarah, Isaac, Jacob, Moses and Miriam, Deborah, King David, the prophets, Jesus, Mary, Peter, Paul, the martyrs and saints, the good men and women who seek to respond to God—just like us. The Bible, the most read and most misused book in the world, is basically a testament to the dialogue between God and the people who try to respond to God. Today, it becomes ours when we understand our stories as the later chapters of that book.

The most fundamental question we must all ask in the pursuit of wisdom is "How can I know that God really is present in my life?"

God and Person

One way we can come to answer this question is through the practice of self-understanding. God is not "out there" and distant; rather, God is the one we discover when we are most ourselves. Psalm 139 is a meditation on the truth of God's presence to the person, and suggests that in our search for God we need look no further than our own lives:

> O LORD, you have searched me and known me.
> You know when I sit down and when I rise up;
>   you discern my thoughts from far away.
> You search out my path and my lying down,

and are acquainted with all my ways.
Even before a word is on my tongue,
O LORD, you know it completely.
You hem me in, behind and before,
and lay your hand upon me.
Such knowledge is too wonderful for me;
it is so high that I cannot attain it.

Where can I go from your spirit?
Or where can I flee from your presence?
If I ascend to heaven, you are there;
if I make my bed in Sheol, you are there.
If I take the wings of the morning
and settle at the farthest limits of the sea,
even there your hand shall lead me,
and your right hand shall hold me fast.
If I say, "Surely the darkness shall cover me,
and the light around me become night,"
even the darkness is not dark to you;
the night is as bright as the day,
for darkness is as light to you.

For it was you who formed my inward parts;
you knit me together in my mother's womb.
I praise you, for I am fearfully and wonderfully made.
Wonderful are your works;
that I know very well.
My frame was not hidden from you,
when I was being made in secret,
intricately woven in the depths of the earth.
Your eyes beheld my unformed substance.
In your book were written
all the days that were formed for me,
when one of them as yet existed.
How weighty to me are your thoughts, O God!
How vast is the sum of them!

I try to count them—they are more than the sand;
    I come to the end—I am still with you . . .

Search me, O God, and know my heart;
    test me and know my thoughts.
See if there is any wicked way in me,
    and lead me in the way everlasting.
(Psalm 139:1b–18, 23–24).

In its essence, this psalm is a prayer of self-understanding, helping us to become aware of the ways in which God has been present to us throughout our lives. It confronts us with the possibility of knowing God not as a distant creator or a holy power in the hands of the elite or a condemning judge or a happy but irrelevant dream. Rather, it draws us into understanding the God who wants to be known to us as the one who has created us for the sheer joy of it. The psalm helps us see the truth phrased by St. Augustine: "You have created us for yourself, Lord, and our hearts are restless until they rest in you."

One important element in the development of self-understanding is the realization that I am not the center of the universe. Those who have studied early childhood development know that the infant is the center of his or her world. As children grow, however, they begin to understand that other people in their lives are not merely servants or appendages of their fancy, but distinct individuals whose lives are not dependent on their own. Further growth, especially in adolescence and adulthood, enables people to understand the world in gradually more expanded ways; people are different, have contrasting viewpoints, and sometimes fight.

Nevertheless, if we are honest with ourselves, we have to admit that we continue to cling, at times, to that infant worldview. It is easy to see those times when we clearly consider ourselves to be rulers of the world, with others serving our needs in minor supporting roles. In this culture, particularly, the cult of individualism is such that we learn to focus on ourselves during the age when we should be learning to focus on others. Focusing on self is not bad, certainly—in fact, it is necessary if we are to find our way in the world as healthy and integrated adults. But it is also important to learn to get beyond self-interest, to relate to other people, because this is the way to happiness. The one who is truly self-centered is miserable.

Self-understanding, then, involves coming to an awareness of our need for others. Real spirituality is not a solitary endeavor; it must reach out beyond the self into that reality which our own faculties of sense and understanding cannot reach. Practically speaking, it involves loving other people. One major reason our generation experiences a loss of meaning is that we have been poorly trained in the discipline (and it is a discipline) of loving. We don't want to "bother" others; we don't want to "infringe" on other people's generosity; we ought to work hard for ourselves; we should mind our own business. Such attitudes, while appropriate at times, cannot be the basis of living in wisdom. For while they do encourage us to work for our own happiness, they do not provide us with the means to achieve it.

There is a deep, organic goodness in being able to do good for another person, even if it requires some suffering on our part. There also is a beauty to allowing others to help us, even if it means allowing ourselves to be in a vulnerable position. When I was in my early teens there was a serious flood to the northwest of Chicago where my family and I lived. About half a block from our house, a creek flowed behind several houses and became a threat to the owners' properties. My dad and I joined the efforts of many others in the neighborhood, throwing sand into bags and lining them up around the threatened homes. The effort lasted hours, with no immediate hope of the water receding. By late in the evening, we had stacked hundreds of sandbags, providing what we considered adequate protection from the flood. We went to bed exhausted, but only after my dad told one homeowner to wake us up immediately if the water continued to rise.

That experience left an impression on me. At no other time during the years we lived in that neighborhood did I encounter so many of our neighbors joining in a common cause to help one another. For a time, I forgot myself to become a part of something greater than myself—and that was a marvelous feeling, especially at that age. It gave me a sense of importance, a desire to do good for other people.

Not long ago I had the experience of needing help myself. I was in San Diego, and decided that the California thing to do was to try in-line skating along the waterfront. During a break, I set off for beautiful

Coronado Island and, for a while, tried to get the hang of it. A couple of minutes into the fiasco, however, I swerved awkwardly and hurt my knee. After a trip to the emergency room, I was given crutches and was told to see an orthopedist as soon as possible.

I was in a fix. My immediate plans had been to fly home to Pittsburgh and then drive out to meet my wife, Sue, at her parents' place in Connecticut. My injury, however, made it impossible for me to drive. I called Sue and told her what was up, thinking maybe I could catch a bus or train when I got to Pittsburgh. During a stopover, though, I received a page over the loudspeaker and went to find that Sue had rearranged my flight so I would arrive in Connecticut, where her dad would pick me up and bring me to their home. I was relieved. I later found out that my great father-in-law was preparing to drive all the way to Pittsburgh to get me, and that only a tremendous effort on Sue's part made it possible for me to re-route my flight to Connecticut. I felt so taken care of, at a time when I really needed the help. I felt pretty stupid the whole time, of course, and just wanted to leave San Diego. Needless to say, I was grateful.

I share these stories because they have helped me understand why self-reliance and individualism aren't enough. Sometimes we need to give; sometimes we must be ready to receive, because only such a disposition allows others to give of themselves. The "golden rule" is an example of an ethical maxim that reveals this two-sided dynamic. We need other people, and other people need us.

But coming to terms with our own hungers for fairness, goodness, mercy, justice, love, and happiness means coming to terms with one very difficult truth: neither I nor other people have all the means to satisfy them. The hardest element in self-awareness is coming to understand the pressing reality of my own suffering, disillusionment, sorrow, helplessness. We have become adept at hiding these things from ourselves, anesthetizing ourselves through work, music, social activities, exercise, or whatever it takes to avoid thinking about our limits. The danger of anesthesia, though, is that it masks the pain which otherwise would be telling us that something is ailing. Unless we feel the distress, we will not get it treated; unless we feel our own suffering, we will not seek salvation. We move so fast that we find it remarkably easy to ignore God completely, a God who speaks in whispers and in silence.

There is a story in the Bible of the prophet Elijah retreating to a cave to wait for the voice of God (see 1 Kings 19:11). There is a fierce wind; but God isn't in the wind. There is a terrible earthquake, but God isn't in the earthquake either. Nor is God in the fire that comes. Rather, God speaks in a tiny whispering voice, which Elijah hears only because he is waiting for God. Today, we often look for God in some dramatic way, expecting that if God is really God then God will dazzle us. But Scripture tells us to pay attention to quiet things if we are to know this God.

Our search for self-understanding must come to terms with the hunger for God, which we experience most acutely when we are still. Because we seek justice, peace, and happiness for ourselves and others, because we seek to end suffering, and because we seek what is good, we seek God. This is the beginning of faith. Christians can recognize in people of all religious persuasions the image of God—the kernel of authentic Christianity is the radical human ability to do what is good, understand what is true, love what is beautiful. The great medieval theologian Thomas Aquinas said it similarly: Whatever is able to love, loves God.

The hunger for God, which is manifested in our desire for the good, the true, and the beautiful, is at the center of who we are as persons. We need an affirmation of who we are, although this need is not always evident. It is like a coach or a teacher who makes clear to us that we are good at something; the feeling "I am good" can be exhilarating. In Christian spirituality, the experience of conversion involves that kind of affirmation of our whole life, our whole self by the God who knows us better than we know ourselves. This is what God's love is like: it magnifies and makes clear to us how very valuable we are to God. And, indeed, God wants to make this clear to us.

Seeking God

Our abilities are small, it is true, and sometimes God is absolutely mysterious. But according to the Judeo-Christian tradition, God is the one who acts first. We need not be theologians in order to find God, because God comes to us. Jesus is God-become-human so that we might be more like God. To seek to know God is to seek to know Jesus and to be like him. But how? He lived a long time ago, in a different place, among different people. What does it mean today, two millennia later, to be like Jesus?

This is not an easy question to answer. To begin with, there are four different stories about the life of Jesus (the Gospels of Matthew, Mark, Luke, and John), and there are the letters written by his early followers (Paul, Peter, John, and others). And although these written sources help us form some ideas about Jesus, they are nonetheless incomplete. Further, the history of those who claim to follow Jesus is varied. For example, there have been controversies and schisms, and differences in belief about who Jesus was and what he called us to do. These problems are about people, though, and not about Jesus; the same problems exist in regard to any major historical figure and his or her message to followers. The challenge to Christians is, as always, to understand and enact the example and teachings of Jesus as best as possible.

An important beginning, then, is to realize that Christian faith is radically a community enterprise. What we understand about God through Jesus has been mediated through the teaching of the Church, a community of human beings that has been fashioned over the ages by the presence of the Holy Spirit. That teaching, although it is general, requires the examples of good men and women to help us understand them in our own lives. From a purely human perspective, we need other people to help us and strengthen us in hard times; it is difficult to live our convictions in an environment in which we are totally alone. And because following Jesus requires that we take seriously the context of his teaching, we must take to heart his teaching that authentic spirituality is both a solitary and a communal pursuit. In his own life, there are times when Jesus withdraws to be alone with the Father in prayer; and there are times when he gathers followers around him, praying and working with them. Ultimately, Jesus' spirituality leads him to reach out to people in need.

Seeking God is a matter of conversion, a shift in our worldview. A catchphrase in the New Testament is "repent and believe the good news" (the Greek word *euangelion,* from which we get our word "evangelize," means literally "good news," translated in English as "gospel"). During the time of Jesus' ministry, people are attracted to him for many reasons: his charisma, his teaching authority, his ability to enter into their lives with compassion and love. His message is constant: conversion. Thus, if we are to understand what Jesus was about, and further what Christian faith seeks to engender in us, we must address the issue of conversion.

Religious conversion involves a shift in our entire experience of life, a shift that can occur only when we are convinced of the new truth. In the case of religious truth, conversion requires the assent of not only reason but also of what is weakly called "the heart." In this sense, it is more like falling in love than agreeing with a proposition. Religious conversion is a coming to awareness that God's love is, indeed, real, and that we have a deep hunger for that love. Jesus' ministry, both in what he does and in what he says, is an effort to convince people of these things. An example is his well-known parable of the prodigal son, in which he describes how God is like a father waiting eagerly for the return of the wayward youth. Jesus describes God as one who desires to be in relationship with each person, but who also recognizes that such a relationship depends on the freedom of the person to choose it.

> Then Jesus said, "There was a man who had two sons. The younger of them said to his father, 'Father, give me the share of the property that will belong to me.' So he divided his property between them. A few days later the younger son gathered all he had and traveled to a distant country, and there he squandered his property in dissolute living. When he had spent everything, a severe famine took place throughout that country, and he began to be in need. So he went and hired himself out to one of the citizens of that country, who sent him to his fields to feed the pigs. He would gladly have filled himself with the pods that the pigs were eating; and no one gave him anything. But when he came to himself he said, "How many of my father's hired hands have bread enough and to spare, but here I am dying of hunger! I will get up and go to my father, and

I will say to him, 'Father, I have sinned against heaven and before you; I am no longer worthy to be called your son; treat me like one of your hired hands.'" So he set off and went to his father. But while he was still far off, his father saw him and was filled with compassion; he ran and put his arms around him and kissed him. Then the son said to him, "Father, I have sinned against heaven and before you; I am no longer worthy to be called your son." But the father said to his slaves, "Quickly, bring out a robe—the best one—and put it on him; put a ring on his finger and sandals on his feet. And get the fatted calf and kill it, and let us eat and celebrate; for this son of mine was dead and is alive again; he was lost and is found!" And they began to celebrate. (Luke 15:11–24)

This parable is rich in its description of the human condition: we want our own way; we want to choose our happiness; we want the power to rule our fate without the responsibility for failure. Only after the son exhausts the resources *which the Father gave him in the first place* does he understand his own hunger, literally and symbolically. This is the moment of conversion. The young man returns to his father freely, ready to enter into a relationship of servitude, but instead is rewarded with a relationship of son to father, with all its joys and satisfactions.

In an anesthetized life, some of us never come to this awareness of our spiritual hunger. Unlike the son in the parable, we remain content to fill ourselves on the "pods" of life (see v. 16), allowing ourselves to live below the dignity with which God endowed us by virtue of our humanity. Conversion does involve coming to our senses, as the young man does (see v. 17)—it is not some magic act apart from our own free will. Like the son, we must choose to enter (again) into relationship with God, a relationship that God already—and always—extends to us in our humanness. God does not, in the gospel parable or in life, give only what is deserved; rather, God gives lavishly, richly, bountifully. God gives a banquet.

Conversion involves a new way of seeing the imprint of God in the world, but in order for such vision to take hold in our lives there must first be a degree of trust that our efforts are not in vain. Like falling in love, conversion is a giving over of ourselves to another; and unless we have some certainty that the beloved will return the gift of self that we take such risk to offer, we will not make a full-hearted effort. It is one thing to love a person from a distance. It is an entirely different thing to summon up the courage to tell that person "I love you."

We can derive assurance of God's eternal love for us in the words of Scripture. We can also look at the history of the Church, at the ways human beings have responded to the call of God in the past, and at the examples of those in our world today who have pledged their lives to the service of God. We can draw from the many expressions of trust in God through prayer and worship across the continents. We can read our own hearts and come to know our desire to love and be loved by God.

There remains, however, the fundamental option of whether to trust that believing in God will give us greater joy. For if Christian faith and spirituality do not make us better human beings, then it is worthless. We are going to reach this banquet of wisdom only by letting the example of Jesus guide our search for God; by following Jesus' examples of word and action; by trying to do in our own lives what Jesus does in his; by responding to the love of God by enacting it in everyday life with others. We can taste for ourselves the promises of a loving God only if we think creatively about how to love like Jesus does—how to love the person next to us or two doors down from us or in the car behind us. We have to reach toward the God who loves us by being students of life and perhaps even students of the Scriptures, since we cannot love someone we do not know.

Ultimately, the practice of spirituality and the experience of conversion are founded on a life of prayer—the meeting place between God and the human soul. It is through prayer that we encounter the Spirit of God, the Spirit promised by Jesus as the one who would be a "comforter" or "advocate" to those who love God. In the Christian tradition, prayer is the beginning of wisdom.

For Group Discussion

1. What experiences of *kairos* have you had, and what have you learned from them?
2. What in your life is most life-giving? What do you live to do? What about this activity makes you happy?
3. What has been your experience of religious authority? What are some positive and negative aspects of the way people use their religious authority?
4. What does "the fear of the Lord is the beginning of wisdom" mean to you?
5. What does prayer mean to you? What, if anything, were you taught as a child about prayer? Do you pray now, and if so, how and why? What kinds of prayer have you found beneficial?

CHAPTER TWO

Food:
God Invites Us to Be Fed
by the Relationship of Faith

Prayer is conversation with God.

—St. Clement of Alexandria

In a movie by the British comedy troupe Monty Python, there is a scene in which a sanctimonious leader prays before a full congregation in a large cathedral: "O God, you are so big . . . you are so very huge . . . gosh, we're all impressed down here!" Sometimes I wonder whether God doesn't regard all our stumbling attempts at prayer as being a bit funny. It seems like many people believe that if they are eloquent and can stand in front of a crowd, they pray well; otherwise, God doesn't care to hear from them!

I'm curious about why so many people feel uncomfortable with the whole idea of praying, especially vocal prayer. They feel they don't know the correct words, they aren't used to it, or they feel awkward. Some of their discomfort, no doubt, may be a simple unease with speaking in front of people. Perhaps, too, it's a matter of what prayer means and whether anyone is listening.

In the movie *It's a Wonderful Life*, George Bailey hits hard times and contemplates suicide on a snow-covered bridge. At this point, he prays in a way that is probably familiar to people who aren't the praying type, basically saying, "I'm not sure you're listening, but I sure need you!" Everyone has times like this, times when we feel helpless and must turn to God. Part of what I find interesting in George Bailey's experience is that he admits that he is not a praying man, and yet he knows, on some level, that he must pray. Many of us are like George; we don't pray all the time, but when trouble comes, God is the one we turn to. I suspect God may be happy with this, even if God would like to hear from us more often.

In *It's a Wonderful Life,* God had been taking care of George, even though George was not aware of it. In turning to God in a time of need, George simply makes himself aware of the presence of God in his life. In other words, prayer helps George, because through George's act of praying, God can respond by sending Clarence the angel to convince George that he does, indeed, have a wonderful life. We all face need in our lives, but many of us speak to God only when our need becomes too much for us to deal with alone. Praying regularly is a form of spiritual maintenance. And just like car maintenance, we pray regularly to avoid problems and to take care of things before they cause a real crisis.

Contemplative Prayer

Some people think that being a person of prayer requires that they renounce all that is illusory in this valley of tears and join a monastery or convent. Indeed, the contemplative vocation is good and holy; but it is a special calling and it is not for everyone. The practice of contemplative prayer, however, is something to which God calls every individual human soul in the context of daily life. It is the response to God's invitation to know God, as expressed in the simple words of Jesus: "Come, follow me."

Contemplation is the name given to that unique form of prayer that seeks communion with the God who calls us into a relationship of love. In contemplative prayer, we acknowledge our strengths and weaknesses, virtues and vices, hopes and fears, recognizing that God accepts us for who we are in that moment of prayer, when, to use Cardinal Newman's phrase, "heart speaks to heart." In contemplative prayer, we open ourselves to God, allowing the Holy Spirit to know our deepest selves, and, in return we grow into a greater awareness of the presence of God.

As young children, many of us learned prayers from the Christian tradition: the Our Father, the blessing before meals, the Sign of the Cross. And, indeed, these are good prayers for us to learn, but unless we come to understand what these prayers mean, they will be little more than recitations of childhood memories. Unfortunately, many of us learned how to *say prayers*, but we never learned to *pray*. Yet, all prayer, and especially contemplative prayer, requires more than just the repetition of words. It is arrogant to believe that God will come around to our way of thinking if our speeches are pretty enough or our incantations sound convincing. On the contrary, words themselves impress God very little. But because we are people of language—we form mental concepts and express ourselves through language—we must begin to pray with language.

We use language in many ways, and so it is helpful to consider the way we use it in prayer. My two-year-old daughter, for example, often will repeat something she hears without really knowing how to use it. She expresses a word, but that word does not really manifest an understanding of a concept. Sometimes people express spoken prayers in a similar way: they repeat what they have heard or read, but the prayer does not touch them on a deeper level. What is important in contemplative prayer is to allow our language to manifest whatever we feel most deeply. It involves reaching below the surface of our language to those mysteries of our lives that are too great for words to adequately express.

Contemplative prayer, then, begins with turning our thoughts toward God, which means turning our minds and, if it helps, our lips to holy things. Psalm 51 has the verse "O Lord, open my lips, / and my mouth will declare your praise." Prayer is never a solitary action, even though it may involve physically removing oneself from the distractions of the everyday world. For prayer involves coming to a greater awareness of the presence of God, a presence that is there always but which we too often ignore. The contemplative seeks a kind of heightened awareness of the ways God moves in his or her life. Frequently it involves the use of Scripture, which is recognized in the Christian tradition as the place where God has self-revealed most clearly (see chapter three). Above all, it means responding to God. It is not a monologue aimed toward God, but attentiveness to the action of God that touches one's deepest self. By using the language of Scripture, we can allow the words to help us become more aware of God, who touches us in ways that language cannot convey.

The simplest form of prayer is silence. In silence, we naturally become reflective, and as contemplatives, we use this reflective space to focus on the presence of God. In today's modern world, the sounds of alarm clocks, radios, televisions, appliances, traffic, and people can become debilitating. Silence helps us restore a kind of equilibrium in the midst of the noise, an awareness of what we need for ourselves. Just as we enter sleep to give our bodies a needed respite from the daily work of living, the experience of silence gives our minds and souls a much needed opportunity for stillness and renewal.

In silence we have greater control of our attention. Too often we use newspapers, magazines, books, television, projects, hobbies, even relationships as ways of "killing time"—and we have become proficient as a culture in inventing new ways of doing this. But are we willing to eliminate the distractions, the time killers, so that silence surrounds us, or does the idea of quiet, alone time actually cause us to feel a measure of angst? We are responsible for the people we create ourselves to be, and without the time to reflect on how we do this, we cannot have a clue as to *who* or *what* we are creating.

Most people sense what I'm referring to. We all experience those times when we need a break, when we need peace and quiet, when we know we're not our best selves because we haven't spent enough time alone. Even our desire to encounter beauty in nature or in art testifies to this spiritual need. Too many of us, however, don't know what we are looking for. I've heard it put this way: we are not human beings who occasionally have spiritual experiences; rather, we are spiritual beings immersed in human experiences. Fundamentally, as spiritual beings, we need God, and in silence, we find God.

The contemplative uses silence to reflect on how his or her life is a gift of God, and to orient his or her life around giving it to God in return. However, the practice of contemplative prayer can be difficult at first. In fact, many who try eventually give up in frustration when "nothing" seems to be happening. This frustration, though, is due, in part, to the expectations people bring into prayer: we should have some kind of "spiritual feeling"; we should feel something profound.[1]

But prayer is part of the fabric of our ordinary living, and, to a great extent, is subject to the same differences of emotion that accompany all our actions. To demand from prayer (and by extension, from liturgical worship) a particular kind of feeling is to place an unreasonable and false expectation upon the dialogue partner: God.

Why Pray?

According to the Letter to the Hebrews, faith is the assurance of things not seen (see 11:1). Since we do not see God in the same way we see much of what goes on in life, we often find it difficult to pray. Sometimes we feel as though we're talking into space, asking for things we'll never get, hoping for things that never happen. And clearly these are real difficulties. Prayer can seem complex, and thus the very act of praying can be an act of faith, even if we think nothing happens and even if we feel no different as a result of having prayed. The answer to the skeptic's question, "Why pray?" is "Prayer is conversation with God," and the only way to know this for sure is to do it.

Those who are not used to praying regularly will do well to consider the comparison of prayer to car maintenance. People who don't know anything about cars may not bother to change the oil or rotate the tires, but eventually these people will experience serious car trouble. Similarly, those who don't pay attention to their spiritual needs will run into trouble. Maybe it will take years, but it will happen. Life is far too complicated for us to assume that we have all the answers, and that our usual way of doing things is enough to satisfy our deepest needs.

For most young men and women, the furthest thing from our minds is death or suffering. We want to enjoy life, meet interesting people, do interesting things; eventually we want to complete our college educations, move into jobs, and have families of our own. Somewhere along the line, however, we're going to come face to face with the reality of pain, suffering, and death. We're going to confront questions of meaning. Prayer is about maintaining a connection to the source of meaning.

Prayer draws us into a deeper understanding of the ways God cares about what we do with ourselves. It is the encounter with meaning in our lives, the encounter with wisdom. It is, among other things, the practice of reminding ourselves that we must seek happiness not only in the everyday things the world offers, but also with the vision of where we have come from, why we are here, and where we are going. It is the chance to know that even in the situations of our lives that crush us, God is there and offering us hope. It is the practice of living life, as opposed to reacting to it.

We may begin contemplation by turning our thoughts to God, just as in a relationship we turn our thoughts to another by asking how the other is doing. In both cases, the object is not specifically *thinking* or *thought*. It is, rather, *presence*. We choose to be with the other, to be with someone we love in silence, and, if we allow it to move us, this presence can be even more powerful than speech. In prayer, we choose to be with God. Certainly, the use of spoken prayers may help "break the ice," as it were, by helping us remove the distractions of the day and focus on the time of prayer. But if we do no more than say a few words and then move on to the next business, it is like walking into a room where your best friend is sitting, reciting a speech, and then leaving. The interpersonal transaction is nil. God wants to be with us, and may even want us to listen, and this requires patience. Our faith grows as we continue to pray, even in the midst of uncertainty. When asked what happened when she prayed, Mother Teresa answered, "I listen to God." When asked what God did during prayer, she replied similarly, "God listens to me."

Prayer, the practice of spirituality, is worth doing because God loves us and wants to be with us. To deny ourselves awareness of the presence of God is like choosing to starve outside the room where Thanksgiving dinner is being graciously served, and for no other reason than we want to be rugged individuals. Prayer is the encounter with the very wisdom that sustains our lives, gives them meaning, makes them rich and worth sharing with others. It is the time when we step out of the rat race to gain a vision of why we even find ourselves in it to begin with. In the experience of prayer, knowing that deep assurance that we are loved by God, we are challenged to do more than just follow along, be part of the crowd, do the same old things that have already been done. We hear and respond to God's invitation to live life as though every moment were a profound gift more valuable than anything (which, by the way, is true).

Through prayer we come to know God, who is like a mirror that reflects not only the soul as it is, but the soul as God has created it, reminding us that the things we do often tarnish the beauty of this original masterpiece. Prayer is thus the chance to take stock of ourselves: to learn what kind of people we are, what kind of people we think we are, what kind of people others think we are, what kind of people we want to be, what kind of people we ought to be. If we are to learn to appreciate how happiness depends on choosing to make ourselves the people we see in the mirror (God), we must be people of prayer. Why pray? We pray that we might encounter reality: the reality of self, the reality of the world in which we live, the reality of those whom we choose to love, the reality of being loved by God. Far from being an escape from the world, prayer is the entrance into the world. Through prayer, we learn to strip away all that is false in ourselves, so that we might more truthfully act in the world to the greater glory of God.

When I was in college, I spent a month traveling through Western Europe, entering and leaving countries in sometimes no more than a few hours. As I traveled, I became keenly aware of how uncomfortable I was in my limited ability to speak to others. My only useful language at the time was Spanish, which did me no good in France, Germany, Italy, or anywhere else besides Spain. At one point I became so frustrated that I decided to head south to Spain, just so I wouldn't feel so isolated! When I arrived, it was so satisfying to talk with travelers from Panama and Madrid. Of course, while I was able to communicate, I did not have the same facility I have in English, so I had to work hard at conversing. But it was worth it.

I mention this story because it points to something most of us don't think about, since language is usually second nature. To some of us, prayer is a foreign language, and because we don't practice it, we feel isolated from God. The human being's natural desire to pray is like my desire to speak to other people: we don't want to be alone. For me, going to a place where I could converse with others was a solace, a comfort, a reminder that I did not have to be all by myself in this tiring journey/pilgrimage through Europe. I humbly realized that being able to communicate with others is a great gift, one I previously had not appreciated.

We talk to people every day, but seldom think about what this gift and privilege actually means. Those who live alone, those who speak a different language, those who have no friends certainly understand; they know the barren loneliness of isolation. They know that we need contact. It has been shown that healthy orphaned babies can die from a condition called "failure to thrive," simply because they receive no attention, no loving touch from another human being. Similarly, healthy elderly people who are left alone can quickly deteriorate without the love of others. These examples remind us of our need to connect with others, and point ultimately to our need for prayer.

Prayer is the language that connects the human heart to God. It is the issuing and receiving of an invitation to enter into a conversation with God, a conversation in which the common language is clearly love.

Daily Prayer

God is a great listener, but that does not make God a magician. Imagine you want to speak to the president of the United States, and by some turn of events you actually get five minutes with him or her. What is the most important thing you can think to say in five minutes? Would you say what a great job he or she is doing or would you get angry and criticize certain policies? Would you use your time to get to know this person or would you ask for something? Many of us are like George Bailey. Our infrequent five minutes with God is all a rush: "I need this. Help!" If we should approach the president with a big request like "Make my birthday a national holiday," because we needed the day off from work, the reply might be: "Um, sorry. I can't do that, at least not right away and not without good reason."

The point is that if we don't learn how to talk to God, we might make unreasonable requests and set ourselves up for disappointment. The regular practice of prayer is like a regular meeting with the president: each person gets to know the other and learns to communicate in a way that works. So when a big issue comes up, it will be much easier to pray, and thereby to know God's love and support, than it would be if we start during a crisis. And by the way, it's easier to pray than to talk to the president. God is always listening.

The simplest kind of prayer is the kind that can be practiced at any time of the day: turning our thoughts to God. Because the contemplative life is guided by the dialogue between God and self, this kind of prayer can take many forms. It can be a simple word of thanks to God before a meal. (The traditional grace before meals is one example of how parents teach children this habit.) It can be an expression of appreciation upon beginning one's day. ("Thank you, God, for your goodness in this day.") It can be an appeal during a difficult situation. ("Lord, help me not to really get time during the day. The point is that we allow God to be present to us throughout the day, and these frequent thoughts help us remember.

It is important, however, that we give ourselves the opportunity to dialogue with God on a deeper level. Personal prayer time set aside enables us to encounter the one who loves us, and to draw from God food for our souls. And just as there are many ways to get together with a friend, so, too, there are many ways to engage in authentic personal prayer: reading Scripture, meditating, making music or creating a work of art, writing, listening to a friend. It is being with God, and allowing God to be with us. The words we say become less important than the attitude we bring to the experience. In the words of Peter, upon witnessing the transfiguration of Jesus: "How good it is to be here!" (Mark 9:5; Matthew 17:4; Luke 9:33) To be with God is to be with the source of life, the source of wisdom. It is through the encounter with God that we can discern the real meaning of our lives and the ways we ought to live.

If we pursue the analogy that our relationship with God is like a deep friendship, it makes sense that it must be sustained by daily communication. Daily life presents us with so much that challenges, stresses, comforts, angers, frustrates, enlightens, and changes us. It can be difficult to really take stock of our lives—some talk about waking up one day and wondering where the last several years have gone. As the days go by, we become different persons, sometimes without even being aware of the change as it is happening. If this can happen to us, then this can affect how we relate even to the dearest of friends. Life changes can happen suddenly, as in graduations or job changes, but they can happen gradually as well. In both cases, we may find that friendships can suffer, even die, if we have not nurtured them with attention on a regular basis.

If prayer is an ongoing relationship with God, we must take responsibility for our side of the relationship—and we do this in the practice of daily prayer. This is an ideal, of course, one which is pursued diligently by professed religious. But it is a difficult ideal for those of us who lead busy lives. Sure, it would be great to have half an hour every day to pray well, but the fact is, with the stresses of today's world, most of us simply do not have this luxury. However, this does not mean that we cannot pray at all.

It is possible to make virtually any good activity a time for prayer, even work itself. We can allow our lives to be suffused with the presence of God, because God is, already and always, everywhere present to us. We simply need to allow our activity to give glory to God by the very fact that God has created us capable of doing it. In the words of St. Irenaeus: "The glory of God is the living human being." Just as an orchestra glorifies a composer when it plays his or her music, or just as children glorify their parents when they make their parents proud, so do people glorify God by doing what they do well. Are you a student? Then glorify God in your diligent study. Are you a tattoo artist? Then glorify God in your careful attention to detail. Do you sing? Are you a good listener? Do you make great coffee? Can you write poetry? Are you able to run a marathon? Have you just started a new job? Do all these things as prayer. Just tell God, "For this you made me; this I do for you."

Work, that which claims perhaps the greatest measure of our time, becomes prayer when we express what God has given us the capacity to do, and when we let this expression be a symbol of thanksgiving. Play, too, becomes prayer when we revel in the goodness of what we are able to do and enjoy doing. Being with friends becomes prayer when we see symbols of the love of God in the friendship we share, recognizing the voice and hand of God in the words and embraces of others. Life itself offers the many opportunities to acknowledge what the Jesuit poet Gerard Manley Hopkins wrote: "The world is charged with the grandeur of God." In different ages, people have seen the hand of God in many ways: in nature, music, the laws of the universe, the moral nature of human living, the hierarchy of living things. When we practice daily prayer, we begin to see the grandeur of God in the world around us. We become adept at the practice of prayer by constantly turning our thoughts to God. And like other kinds of practice, the rewards of prayer develop over time.

Organized Religion

Many people today don't "do" religion. They may consider themselves spiritual, they may even pray regularly, but they find religion restrictive and old-fashioned. Some create a kind of spiritual collage by borrowing rituals and practices from other traditions: they may pray the rosary, do yoga, get in touch with their inner child, study the martial arts, or beat drums to get in touch with the rhythms of nature.

There is a division in the way this culture views organized religion. On the one hand, there are those who have been raised in a particular religious tradition, who recognize in that tradition certain values such as a moral upbringing for children and a place for the development of community, a place to reflect on spiritual truths. On the other hand, there are those who view organized religion with suspicion, perhaps because they perceive some political or social agenda or because they have been disillusioned with its hypocrisy. In the postmodern age, the issue of organized religion has become so charged that it is seldom a topic of polite conversation. How can we reconcile these differing visions? Specifically, how should organized religion fit into a vision of authentic Christian spirituality?

Organized Christianity began in apostolic times and has been an important historic part of the practice of Christianity. We see especially in the Acts of the Apostles and in the New Testament letters that the early followers of Jesus struggled with the social problems of shared faith—problems such as how to share money and resources, who the authentic authority figures were, which understanding of Jesus was right, how to pray, who was admitted into worship. Christians today still struggle with these complex issues. Those who call for a return to the "old way" of doing things in the Church are often wishing for a Church that actually never existed; even Peter and Paul had their disagreements. This fact, however, does not mean that Christians through the ages were not sincere in their faith.

I begin with this observation to highlight the fact that the Church is, first of all, a complex human institution (and by *Church* here I mean somewhat ambiguously the group of people who follow Jesus). Although its aim is divine, the Church is always human, subject to the same problems as other human institutions. It is sometimes led by inept people; it sometimes undergoes bad times; it sometimes makes poor financial decisions. It experiences tension within the ranks, and sometimes there are differences between the leaders and the followers. Certain members sometimes act hypocritically, inflicting emotional or physical harm on different groups of people.

The above criticisms, however, are applicable to virtually any large institution and do not represent problems unique to the Church. Rather, these imperfections reflect problems inherent in any human community. The reason such problems are especially scandalous in the Church is that we expect it to be better. If the aim of Christianity is the worship of God, then the aim of the Church must be to act in ways that glorify God.

Why, though, must we bother with organized religion if the aim of spirituality is communion with God? Isn't it possible to be spiritual persons, committed to prayer and good action, without having to "go to church" on Sunday?

These questions are common among seekers of faith. To be sure, there are many good people who, for one reason or another, have rejected the idea of organized religion to pursue spirituality on a more individual basis. While it is laudable to value personal spirituality, community prayer (and therefore organized religion) is also important. Private prayer alone leaves one at risk of becoming too self-focused. To be like Jesus means being other-focused: loving God through the practice of loving the neighbor. Private spirituality ought to help us make personal (and habitual) what is essentially a public matter: how we are to love others. In other words, our personal spirituality and spiritual community membership and participation complement each other.

The life of Jesus is an example of this: there are times when Jesus withdraws to be alone with the Father (like his forty days in the desert or his agonizing hours in the Garden of Gethsemane), but the greater part of his ministry, according to the Gospels, is spent in public, among the people. If authentic Christianity means imitating Jesus, then authentic Christian spirituality is not exclusively personal. It is not only an exercise through which we give ourselves more peaceful, stress-free lives or connect with the world beyond that of our senses. It cannot be only an attempt to know things other people don't. Rather, Christian spirituality is the practice of a wisdom founded on the love of God for people, a love that must be made concrete by our actions in the world, motivated by our desire to love God in return. Private prayer is but one movement in this dynamic.

We need organized religion, in spite of its limitations (and the frustrations we may have with other people), because we need to be part of the worshiping community that celebrates, remembers, and makes present the love of God poured out through Jesus Christ by the power of the Holy Spirit. Practically speaking, we need the Church because individually we are limited. We need the Church because we need to be challenged, reminded, and exhorted. We need the Church, for it is here that we encounter others who are motivated to understand the presence of God in their lives.

This last point is critical. Understanding how to live a good life is difficult; understanding the movements of the Holy Spirit is difficult. If we rely only on our own abilities to discern God's word, we run the risk of equating God's will with our own. The Church offers that meeting place where we encounter other people who struggle with faith, who can help us understand our own struggle. Perhaps more importantly, a community of the faithful helps us recognize that faith demands the questioning of our own understanding of God, which is always limited.

Perhaps the most common problem with organized religion is the practice of "going to church." For so many people, attending church regularly is tedious, even meaningless. The solution, however, is not the avoidance of church altogether, but the improvement of the ways Christians choose to celebrate and express their faith. This has always been one of the great struggles within individual churches, and it can be accomplished only if there are people committed to making "church" better. Certainly, many churches do it right. I've been to some fantastic churches and know that when worship is done well, it is a magnificent experience that ranks up there in pure emotional appeal with a good concert or athletic event (with different objectives in each case, of course). When "church" is done well, the experience of celebrating and worshiping together enables people to encounter the presence of God.

The idea of "organized religion" may gain greater respect if the community focuses on the *meaningful celebration of its liturgies* and a *mature understanding of its teaching* .

Meaningful liturgy. In his instructive work *Encyclopedia of Catholicism*, Richard McBrien explains that liturgy is "the public and official prayers and rites of the Church. The term signifies that worship is an activity of the whole Church, laity and clergy alike." The word *liturgy* comes from a Greek word that means "worship," but its roots are two other words that, literally translated, mean "people work." The etymology of the word is suggestive of a key point in what makes liturgy good: the contributions of the worshiping community. Liturgy is powerful when it enables God-seeking people to know God through their combined efforts.

How is liturgy different from private prayer? The difference lies in the very fact that liturgy is a community endeavor, an effort of the people. It is the difference between a violin solo and a symphony; between shooting hoops alone and playing a five-on-five, full-court basketball game; between a single person picking up trash off the street and an entire community participating in a clean-up day. The combined effort of a community is a magnificent thing to behold, under any circumstance. When that effort is dedicated to the praise of God, though, the human effort is, at the same time, a divine effort. The human community, the crown of God's work, reflects its own desire to do what it was created by God to do.

The experience of meaningful liturgy puts us in touch with being part of something bigger than ourselves, of self-transcendence. It is an encounter with what is truly great about the human condition: the ability to come together in ways that supersede anything we can do as individuals. We know this expansion of the human spirit in other types of endeavors: the Olympics, for example, or championships or presidential elections or international celebrations like New Year's Eve. We know this same fullness in our local communities as well, when we respond to the needs of a family who lost everything in a home fire, or give blood when the Red Cross issues an alert that blood banks are low. The satisfaction we experience is due to our recognition and celebration of what is best in us. Liturgy, when it is done well, is a moment in this celebration—but it celebrates even more profoundly the work of God which makes it all possible. Good liturgy helps us know *how* God makes this possible, by reflecting on the work of God throughout human history, but particularly in the ministry of Jesus.

While this represents the ideal of liturgy, the reality for many of us is nowhere near it. If good liturgy is like Handel's *Alleluia* chorus, many of us are left with nothing more than bad elevator music. But bad liturgy or good liturgy is not something that happens *to* us; rather, liturgy is what we *make* of it. We experience meaningful liturgy when we choose to make it so by claiming it as our own. True, many churches rely on centuries-old rituals, prayers, and songs, but these can be magnificent when they are appropriated by modern people. One obvious example is the Lord's Prayer: it was composed some two thousand years ago, but its relevance and ability to touch people have not diminished over time. Ancient ways of worshiping need not become outdated if they enable us to turn ourselves toward God, but this can happen only if we make the effort to understand them. The language of the psalms is another example: they were written centuries before Christ, but in different ages they have been set to modern music so that they might be prayed in ever new ways.

An example of an extended worshiping community that has tried to appropriate ancient ways of praying is the monastic community at Taizé, France. This community of Catholic and Protestant monks prays every day with literally thousands of people, especially teens and young adults, using the form of chant as a way to meditate on the work of the Holy Spirit. There is nothing new going on here—the words are biblical and the chant is basically the same as has been used for a thousand years—but the monastic community uses these ancient forms of praise in ways that are meaningful to the gathered community. Many people from around the world, young and old, gather at Taizé for retreats and pilgrimages, and carry their style of prayer back home. Today there are many churches in the United States that practice Taizé-style worship.

Teaching. Liturgy is one good reason we need organized religion. A second one is teaching. Christian teaching, or doctrine, has developed over two thousand years and therefore is richer and more complex than any of us can appreciate alone. Even those of us who spend our lives studying the tradition of Christian doctrine recognize that we need a community in order to better appreciate what it means for us today. One major reason there is such a long development of Christian doctrine is that it is based in our understanding of the Bible, an enormously difficult collection of texts. As early as the time of Paul, there were differences of opinion on what Christians should believe about Jesus. Paul himself counseled that it was important to maintain unity:

> Now I appeal to you, brothers and sisters, by the
> name of our Lord Jesus Christ, that all of you be
> in agreement and that there be no divisions among
> you, but that you be united in the same mind and
> the same purpose (1 Corinthians 1:10).

Today, there are still many divisions about what it means to be a follower of Jesus. It is a mistake to believe that any one person has all the answers. We must follow Paul's advice, and not allow our differences of belief obscure the more important matter of being united with one another in community.

There are different kinds of teaching in the Church, but one example will highlight why we need the church community to grow in our understanding and practice of faith. In recent years, many people have raised questions about when it is right to stop medical treatment for people who are terminally ill. Relatively speaking, this is a recent question in the development of humankind; there are no clear answers in the Bible, for medical technology has developed beyond what the biblical authors understood. Many Christians have sought to shed light on this question by appealing to biblical concepts, such as God being the author of life, or the resurrection of the dead. Their use of these concepts, together with their understanding of medicine and law, show a great deal of creativity and thoughtfulness. They manage to apply what they value through their faith to the difficult moral questions surrounding terminal illness.

People who confront this issue for the first time can draw from the wisdom of others who have studied it in detail. They can learn about how other people of faith have wrestled with this same issue, and thus become better equipped for the moral decisions they will face. In other words, they do not have to go it alone; they do not have to face the paralysis of not knowing what to do, because they can appeal to a body of teaching. They can learn how to apply what they believe to a difficult issue that eludes easy answers. And because they can do this, they can grow in their faith.

Christian doctrine can seem like a heavy burden to those who do not understand it, but it is helpful to think of it as the ongoing conversation between people of faith about what that faith means. We need this tradition so that we avoid the mistakes our predecessors made. We also need it to challenge us to understand and practice our faith in new ways.

. . .

Becoming people of prayer means that we are willing to challenge our understandings of ourselves, others, and God. What begins as a desire to make our lives more meaningful will develop into a need to connect with other people who share this desire. Contemplative prayer naturally leads to organized religion, which is founded on the biblical tradition.

In the next chapter, we look at how the Bible helps us in our prayer, in our desire to grow closer to the God who is the source of wisdom. First we ask what it means to say that the Bible is the revealed Word of God. Next we look at the different types of writings found in the Bible, and explore how we must therefore read them in different ways. Finally we focus on two types of readings: story and spirituality.

For Group Discussion

1. Is God present to you in your life? What experiences have led to your conviction?
2. How has your understanding of God changed as you've matured? What factors have contributed to this change?

3. How has an experience of spiritual crisis changed your beliefs about God?
4. Do you have periods of silence in your daily routine? How do you feel in silence? What does this observation tell you about yourself?
5. How can you transform what you do in daily life into acts of prayer?
6. What experiences of liturgy have you found moving? What made that experience different? How did it "speak" to you?

Nourishment: God Nourishes Us with God's Word

Scripture is like a river in which both the lamb can wade and the elephant can swim.

—St. Gregory the Great

The quotation above, written at the end of the sixth century by the famous pope and Doctor of the Church, says something about why the Bible has been such a foundational document in the life of the Church. On a basic level, the Bible is filled with interesting stories about God and people, stories that tell us things about the human condition and about the ancients' understanding of God's work. At deeper levels, however, Scripture challenges us with basic questions about ourselves, our tendency toward evil, and the sometimes bizarre and troubling aspects of divinity. The Bible also provides colorful children's stories and stories of sexual immorality, genocide, and slavery. To read it only at face value is to avoid confronting these more difficult issues.

For various reasons, there seems to be a general unfamiliarity with the Bible, even among many churchgoing people. Some people have never really read it since their childhood, when they learned some of the stories about Moses, David, and Jesus. Others know certain selections they have heard many times in church but have never considered them in the larger context of the Bible as a whole. Then there are those who read the Bible faithfully every day, but perhaps have never learned much about its history, its authors, or its original readers. We must remember, of course, that for the majority of the Church's history to date, most Christians were either illiterate or unable to acquire a text of the Bible for personal reading. The Bible was first a document to be read aloud, as it is in churches today. And since the Bible has been and is the focal point of Christian spirituality, the Church has always gathered together to hear the proclamation of and preaching on Scripture.

More and more, though, individual Christians (and even non-Christians) must understand what the Bible is about if they are to consider themselves serious spiritual seekers. As ordinary Christians become more educated and politically powerful, they face greater and greater moral responsibilities, the responses to which must be informed not only by intelligent reflection but also by prayer. In recent years, for example, many political elections have involved difficult issues that divide even devout believers. If authentic Christian spirituality is biblical, it is important that Christians know what the Bible does and does not say.

What Exactly Is the Bible?

To declare that "the Bible says *x*" is not much clearer than insisting that "the library says *x*." The Bible is a collection of different books in which there is no linear progression from beginning to end and no systematic argument throughout. Because the voice of God can come only through human language, we must ask questions about that language, especially that which was written so long ago. The Bible as we know it came together over centuries of writing, editing, and collecting. The oldest writings were probably transcriptions from oral traditions that may date back to the millennium before Jesus was born; the later writings were set down in the early second century after Jesus. In the late fourth and early fifth centuries C.E., forty-six books of what we call the Old Testament, and twenty-seven books of what we call the New Testament were recognized by church councils in the north of Africa, and were gradually established as the *canon* (measure) of the Christian Bible. The Catholic and Orthodox churches accept this fourth-century canon, while Protestant churches accept only the thirty-nine books of the Old Testament, which comprised the Hebrew Bible established in the first century C.E.[1]

This short history offers us insight into why it is difficult to read and understand the Bible. Since the different books were written in such varying circumstances, we must know something about those different circumstances if we are going to understand what the books are about. Consider one example: just as we would be mistaken to read a newspaper the same way we would read a science-fiction novel, so too would we be mistaken to read all the books of the Bible in the same way. One basic question then is, What kind of writing are we reading? Is it history, poetry, myth, or moral exhortation?

One modern example will make clear why it is important to understand something about the different kinds of biblical literature. When Orson Welles' radio play *The War of the Worlds* was first broadcast, it caused great panic. This is a story about Martians landing on earth and destroying the world. Many people heard it, but tuned in unaware that it was a work of fiction. When they learned that Martians were destroying the world, they thought it was fact, and they were horrified. A simple statement would have allayed these listeners' fears: "This is fiction! It's not fact!"

When some people read the Bible, a similar dynamic takes place. They think they are reading something totally different than what the author actually intended to convey. To address this problem, biblical scholars try to make sense of these texts. They try to remind us, for example, that the Book of Revelation was not written to forecast the future but rather to remind second-century Christians that God ultimately is in charge, using highly symbolic language that people of the day would have understood.

Perhaps the most difficult issue people must wrestle with in confronting biblical text is the belief that the Bible is revelation. For Christians, the Bible represents a meeting point between human and divine: God speaks to humans through the words of the biblical text. It is precisely this point which Christians take for granted, and non-Christians find bewildering. Just what does it mean to claim that the Bible is revelation?

First, let us examine what this claim does not mean. Biblical revelation does not mean that God personally wrote the words in heaven and presented a complete book to some important religious figure. It does not mean that the biblical writers were possessed by the Spirit of God to the extent that they did not know what they were writing, as one might envision a ghost taking over someone's body. It does not mean that all the words of the Bible are so undeniably clear to the person of faith that those who do not understand must be evil in some way. And while I doubt that anyone would make these claims, I sometimes suspect that people talk about the Bible as if one or more of these were the case.

To claim that the Bible is revelation (i.e., God's "self-revealing" to people) is to recognize that we can find in these writings by human beings inspired by faith in God truths about the relationship between God and people, and about the human condition. Practically, then, this means that when the biblical writers sought to convey their understanding of God's work in human history, they drew from the stories of people who were convinced of the reality of God in their midst. These stories often were based on historical events like the Exodus from Egypt or the Exile in Babylon. In other cases, they were attempts to explain how the world order developed from God's creative activity, like parts of Genesis and the Psalms, for example. In still other cases, these stories sought to address God directly, rendering praise and thanksgiving to God, or crying out to one who might understand the suffering of the innocent, like parts of Exodus or Jeremiah.

Biblical revelation explores the range of the human situation and the attempts through history to understand how God fits into it all. It gives us insights into how people thousands of years ago confronted some of the same questions we wrestle with today: Why is there evil? Where did the world come from? Why do I exist? What ought I do to have life? Who is God? It makes us sometimes painfully aware of the reality of the human condition, but it also offers us the hope that our sufferings are not meaningless.

Above all, the Bible is revelatory because it is the testimony (or testament) of people who have encountered the living God in an utterly profound way. The theme that holds the Bible together is that God has worked—and continues to work—in the midst of humanity. The Old Testament recalls the origins of God's creativity and how God chose to self-reveal to Abraham and his descendants, establishing with them a "covenant," an agreement between parties: "I will be your God, and you will be my people" (Exodus 6:7). It tells how God self-revealed to Moses, empowering him to lead Israel into a free land, so beautifully described by Miriam. It describes the history of Israel and gives us insight into how that nation understood the origin of the world and their place in it. It gives us the wisdom writings of Israel and their prayers to God, as well as the extended writings of the prophets, those who constantly reminded Israel not to forget the God who led them to freedom.

The New Testament is organized around the historical figure Jesus of Nazareth, giving accounts of his words and deeds and reflecting on what he taught. In the New Testament we encounter what is the most profound claim of Christianity: God became human, lived among us for a time, and taught us what it means to be truly human. Christian belief and practice comes out of the conviction that Jesus is the "anointed" one of God (Greek *Christos,* Hebrew *Messiah*), the one who not only points to the work of God but also is, in his very person, the incarnation (Latin: "taking flesh") of God. In Jesus, Christians believe, God's love for humankind is more than just a hopeful reminder: it is a historical reality.

The early followers of Jesus, even before they were called *Christians*, wrestled with who Jesus was and what his teaching meant. We see in the Gospels, for example, the scene in which Jesus confronts Peter (see Matthew 16:13–17): "Who do you say that I am?" Peter's response, "You are the Messiah," gives words to the basic convictions of these early followers. Now, as then, to be a follower of Jesus means sharing this conviction. Practically it means believing the testimonies of the biblical witnesses. More profoundly, however, it means seeing in the teachings of Jesus and the stories about Jesus the truth of God's intimate love for the individual person. To be a Christian is to understand at some level that Christ died for each of us. It is to appreciate that although there is great suffering in the world, Christ shares in our suffering because he was not exempt from it. It is to believe, sometimes with difficulty, that God says to us: *You are not alone.*

For some, this conviction comes easily because it is the natural conclusion to which they are led through life experience growing up in a religious community. For others, though, it is difficult to assert, with any clarity and certainty, that Jesus was anything more than a wise man who taught powerfully. Young people especially consider this second claim, because of the difficulty they face in trying to reconcile the truth claims about Jesus and the truth claims of other faith traditions. To be sure, this difficulty has a long history. Many early followers of Jesus were challenged to reconcile the teachings of Jesus with those of other religious traditions, debating whether Jesus was really God or merely someone who was wise. One of the early Latin Christian writers, Tertullian, wrestled with the radical nature of the truth claims of Christianity, judging that the credibility of the faith lay in the fact that it seemed so incredible: "I believe because it is absurd."

Those of us in Gen2K are suspicious about truth claims in general, and so it isn't enough to simply say "This is what the Church teaches about Jesus. Believe it!" We need to know for ourselves who Jesus is. In this way, we are like the character Thomas in John's Gospel, who heard about the Risen Jesus from others, but wouldn't believe it until he had seen for himself. What is interesting in that story, and which applies to us, is that Jesus is happy to oblige. "See for yourself," he basically says, as if to imply that this desire to know him is good even when it involves a bit of doubt. Many of us have doubt, of course, but our doubt can (paradoxically) lead us to ask the right questions about faith. It can be the impetus for us to seek to understand Jesus, and thereby to better understand who God is.

Christian spirituality is not only something to think about rationally, however; it is a practice that develops over time. Christian faith cannot ultimately be proven (although it can be rationally reflected upon), but it *can* be experienced. Over the centuries, Christian witnesses have pointed to a single theme: God's love for us is real. The only way to know the truth of Christian spirituality is to just do it. Faith develops out of the dynamic between doubt and conviction. *Doubt* arises from our desire to know things for sure, understanding that spiritual truths are different from scientific ones. *Conviction*, however, grows slowly through accepting as true the stories about God, and the understanding of our own experiences as being related to these stories. The Bible becomes not only a collection of books but a living record of stories to which we can compare our own stories. Is it true that God led the Israelites out of Egypt? If so, then isn't it possible that God has led others out of their slavery? And then doesn't it stand to reason that God can lead me to greater freedom in my life?

When read through the eyes of faith, the Bible becomes a rich source of revelation. Stories, prayers, and the teachings of Jesus become examples of how to make sense of our own lives. Rather than representing only ancient ways of understanding the world, Scripture becomes a timeless reminder of God's presence throughout history. When reading about the promises of God to his people, we can take delight in being included in the promise:

> Ho, everyone who thirsts, come to the waters;
>   and you that have no money, come, buy and eat!
> Come, buy wine and milk
>   without money and without price.
> Why do you spend your money for that which is not bread,
>   and your labor for that which does not satisfy?
> Listen carefully to me, and eat what is good,
>   and delight yourselves in rich food.
> Incline your ear, and come to me;
>   listen, so that you may live (Isaiah 55:1–3).

Such a biblical text becomes an invitation to the banquet of wisdom, describing those who have already shared it and showing them how to participate as well. The problem for many, however, is that they have not the means to believe that the Bible is revelatory, even though they may recognize that it is an important source of human history and moral teaching. For such people, responding to Jesus' invitation to "come and see" can be the beginning of a nurturing feast.

How Can We Make Sense of the Bible?

How are we to read the Bible as a source of Christian spirituality? Simply open it and start reading. Somewhat surprisingly, there are many people (even people of faith) who never do this personally, thus limiting their knowledge of Scripture to what they glean from their worship experiences. It is important that we understand for ourselves what the Bible says. To put it more simply, the biblical text can become the place where God addresses our hearts directly.

There are times when people simply let the Bible fall open to a certain place, then read the first things they see, concluding that this is how God would speak to them. One famous example is that of St. Augustine, who heeded the mysterious voice of a child exhorting him to "take and read" the first text he saw. Augustine records the event in his autobiography, *Confessions*, noting that it was this experience of reading the first text he laid eyes on that was the final decisive factor in his conversion to Christianity. While I do not discount that this kind of experience can be revelatory, and has been for many people, it is not the kind of experience with the Bible that everyone can expect. The spirituality that develops out of our encounter with the Bible comes from much perseverance and hope.

Although there are many ways to approach the biblical text, ways that become easier with practice, here we explore two. Perhaps the simplest and most obvious is to read the Bible as a series of stories. Certain texts are better for this manner of reading: for example, the first creation story of Genesis 1, the Exodus account, or the gospel narratives about Jesus' life. A second way to read the Bible is to approach it as a source for one's own prayer. The Psalms, for example, give us profound language for turning ourselves to God.

The following sections use texts from both the Old and the New Testament as examples of how the biblical text is a rich source of wisdom for Christians. These sections are examples of biblical interpretation.

The Bible as Story

Genesis 1: Since the time of Darwin, there has been considerable debate about the truth of the Genesis account of creation. Some claim that Genesis is a literal account of the beginning of the world; others tend to be more scientific, offering physical evidence that leads them to conclude that the world is far older than the seven or eight thousand years calculated by the "biblicists." How do we reconcile this debate?

Simply put, there is no conflict between the Genesis creation stories and the evidence of science. Modern biblical criticism has led a majority of scholars to recognize that the authors of Genesis 1–3 (there are at least two authors, separated by centuries) never intended to give a historical account. What they do give us, however, is fascinating and deeply insightful about the human condition and about God. Many use the term *myth* to describe these creation accounts. Instead of being a negative term ("that's just a myth"), though, use of the word *myth* in this context refers to a literary style characterized by the use of imagery, personification of God, etiology (the explanation of the origins of things), and metaphor, to name a few. Genesis 1–3 may not tell us about the exact beginning of the universe, but it does tell us about God and ourselves.

Chapter one of Genesis comes from roughly the sixth century B.C.E., produced by a person or group (called the "Priestly" source, since it was likely that they were part of the Israelite religious establishment) living in exile from Israel. The story shows God as the creator, the one who is in charge of the entire human destiny across history. This theology would have been reassuring to those who were exiled from their homeland. This God is portrayed as an artist, one whose creative activity springs from the simple joy of creating. The artist takes delight in what he has created: "God saw everything that he had made, and indeed, it was very good" (1:31).

The portrayal of God as an artist is enormously rich. On one level, it tells us of God's presence in all of the created order, from the subatomic lepton to the macrocosmic stretches of space. As an author is always present in a text, or a composer in a piece of music, so is God present in all creation. This basic belief in God's creativity has led countless people throughout human history to turn their thoughts to divinity upon encountering beauty: a sunset, a starry night, a mountain. There is, one might say, a primitive instinct that leads us to an experience of awe in the face of intense beauty, as if the human heart is inscribed with a need to express thanksgiving. For the Israelite author(s), the encounter with creation was an encounter with God. This sentiment is echoed in the language of the even older Psalm 19 (c. eleventh to tenth century B.C.E.): "The heavens are telling the glory of God."

It is fascinating that the Priestly source writes that the human being was the last part of creation:

Then God said, "Let us make humankind in our image, according to our likeness; and let them have dominion over the fish of the sea, and over the birds of the air, and over the cattle, and over all the wild animals of the earth, and over every creeping thing that creeps upon the earth.

So God created humankind in his image,
in the image of God he created them;
male and female he created them.

God blessed them, and God said to them, "Be fruitful and multiply, and fill the earth and subdue it; and have dominion over the fish of the sea and over the birds of the air and over every living thing that moves upon the earth." (Genesis 1:26–28)

To say that human beings are created in the image and likeness of God is to make profound claims. First, it means that God has taken special care in the creation of human creatures, endowing them with the gift of "Godhood." Second, it means that people have a nobility in the very fact that they are human, and so like God: this is the main thing that sets us apart from animals. This second point is the foundation for the belief that Christians are to serve even the poorest, most excluded, most unprotected human beings. For if all human beings—rich or poor, black or white, male or female, mentally ill or physically handicapped, born or unborn, elderly or young, addicted or infected, gay or straight—are by their very existence created in the image of God, then they are the object of God's love.

A third point we can draw from the Priestly source is the surprising emphasis (for the time it was written) that male and female alike were created with the same dignity. Modern feminist Christian writers have sought to build on this point, one that has received comparatively little treatment in the religious traditions of Judaism and Christianity. In this account, neither the man nor the woman has dominance over the other. Rather, both are charged with the task of being "fruitful," and taking care of the good things of the earth. Both are the recipients of God's gifts.

Finally, the fact that God rests on the seventh day of creation reflects the Priestly observation of the Sabbath. Although the Sabbath institution was not formalized until the covenant with Moses, even here the Priestly author suggests that rest, since it was integral to creation itself, is a necessary element in human living. Orthodox Judaism still observes the Sabbath with utmost seriousness, while Christians vary in their understanding of what it means. For many, it is a reminder to join with the worshiping community. For others, it is a day to spend with family and friends. It is worth considering, in a fast-moving society like ours, why we need rest. The text says that God made the seventh day holy *because* he rested, as if to suggest that rest from good work is itself a holy thing. For many, this is hard to believe. We have to work for grades, work to find a job, to get ahead, to get time off, to provide for our families, to plan for retirement. Don't we have to work for spirituality? for wisdom? This text suggests otherwise. To be created in the image of God, to be like God, means that our very existence "declares the glory of God," even more than the firmament of heaven and the rest of creation.

This point ought to give us some comfort. To be human, to be created in the image and likeness of God, means sharing in the very goodness of God. This God, whose resting makes the day holy, has given to human beings the same need for rest, and in our resting we mirror the divine image. We need not do anything to be like God! In theological language, we stand before God already as recipients of grace. The word *grace* is related to the Latin word *gratis*, which means "free," as in a gift that is given for nothing. To be a recipient of grace, then, means to have been given God's gift of God's own self—not as a reward for work already done but as the free expression of divine creativity.

Too often we connect moral goodness or worth with certain kinds of behavior, patterns we learn as children: "Do the right thing." Reflection on God's creativity, however, reminds us that even before we act, we are inherently good because we are the unique objects of God's love and delight. To be loved by God is simply *to be*. We need not earn God's favor. On the contrary, it is futile to try to do anything to earn God's love. To be human is to be a testament to God's creative work, and thus everything that human beings do as expressions of this humanity is further testament.

Matthew 26–28: The Gospel according to Matthew is a story about a Jewish man whose life fulfills ancient Jewish prophecies about the kingdom of God. Matthew, who probably used some of the stories found in the earlier Gospel according to Mark, was trying to show his fellow Jews that Jesus of Nazareth was the one about whom Micah, Isaiah, Jeremiah, and other ancient prophets wrote centuries earlier. In his account of the death of Jesus, written around 70–80 C.E. (about forty or fifty years after Jesus), Matthew notes some remarkable things.

The passion account in Matthew's Gospel is a story of a Jesus who heroically accepts his role as described by the prophets, and who, in fulfillment of their words, goes to his death for the sake of his people. In the first two lines of chapter 26, we see a foreshadowing of this story: Jesus predicts his own crucifixion two days before it happens. Here Matthew presents a Jesus who is fully aware of who he is and what he must do. This is no ordinary man. Having taught about God, the kingdom of heaven, and the last judgment, Jesus knows he has a particular task before him, and he must suffer through it for the sake of all humanity.

This theme is highlighted again in the story about the woman at Bethany (see Matthew 26:6–13). Jesus is at the home of a diseased man, continuing his ministry to the outcasts of Israel. The woman anoints Jesus with expensive oil, and his response is telling:

> "For you always have the poor with you, but you will not always have me. By pouring this ointment on my body she has prepared me for burial. Truly I tell you, wherever this good news is proclaimed in the whole world, what she had done will be told in remembrance of her."
> (Matthew 26:11–13)

Matthew's Jesus seems to have a perfect understanding of his role in history, as if to say that every move he makes has the import of being recorded permanently on a CNN newsreel.

Matthew frequently mentions that Jesus does something to fulfill a prophecy, and often makes reference to Jewish practices that would be known only to Jews. It is not unreasonable to suggest, then, that

Matthew is addressing Jewish readers. Clearly, he was enormously moved by Jesus (the very fact that he wrote anything, in a time when writing was uncommon, testifies to this). Even more, though, Matthew saw in the words and actions of Jesus something of God himself—the same God who, we may guess, Matthew learned about as a Jew, the God of the ancient figures Abraham, Isaac, Jacob, and Joseph. A Jew who made this kind of claim, risking blasphemy and the punishment of death, had to have very strong reasons for doing so. In short, Matthew was absolutely convinced that Jesus was the Messiah, the one called by God himself to save his people of Israel.

The idea of a Messiah gradually arose in the prophetic literature of Israel and developed over centuries. While there is no clear description in the Old Testament of what the Messiah would be like, there were different ideas around the time of Jesus. One general view held that the Messiah would be a conqueror, restoring to Israel the glory it held under King David. Matthew, in fact, writes that there was a direct lineage from David to Jesus, hinting that Jesus is the fulfillment of David's kingdom. But as Matthew's story develops, we see him wrestling with a different notion of the Messiah, one to which there were allusions in the books of the prophets like Isaiah and Jeremiah. This notion offered that the Messiah would be one of humble birth, whose ministry would be to demonstrate God's loving concern for his people, and whose life would be one of suffering. For Matthew, Jesus is this person. Jesus' life is shown to be one of complete self-giving, to the point of his death.

Matthew's story of the Last Supper exemplifies this attitude. Jesus gives thanks (Greek *eucharisto*, from which we get the word *eucharist*) to God for the gifts of bread and wine. But in a rather enigmatic way, he shares them with his followers only after pronouncing that they now carry a new meaning: "This is my body," and "This is my blood." Matthew's audience would have understood readily the reference he makes in 26:27–28: "Then he took a cup, and after giving thanks he gave it to them, saying, 'Drink from it, all of you; for this is my blood of the covenant, which is poured out for many for the forgiveness of sins.'"

The covenant (some texts read "new" covenant) refers to God's agreement with Abraham, which was ratified through the sacrifice of animals. In Hebrew worship, the Feast of Atonement, or God's forgiveness, was celebrated with the use of a "scapegoat," an animal upon whom the entire community would ritually place its sins. The scapegoat would be killed, thus ritually putting to death the sins of the community, and its blood would be smeared upon the altar of sacrifice. Jesus is referring to this gruesome practice, suggesting that it is he who will become the "new" scapegoat for humanity. As the Son of God (a term Matthew uses in several places), it is he who can accept the sins of the world in a way a ritual animal cannot, and through his death, sins are not only ritually forgiven, they are actually forgiven. Matthew alone among the Gospels adds the key phrase "for the forgiveness of sins" to his account of the Last Supper to emphasize this point.

Clearly, Matthew suggests that Jesus' action is a way of changing the way his followers understood God's forgiveness. Jesus' gift of himself is God's way of reaching out to people, of helping them to know the reality of love through the very sacrifice of an only son. For the early Christians, the fact that Jesus dies so horribly is a source of confusion. But the story of the Last Supper in all four Gospels suggests that Jesus knows his death will happen, and further suggests that he intends it to be an event that will carry meaning: Jesus loves his people so much that he is willing to die for them. And through his death, the Evangelists tell us, God demonstrates a personal love for the world.

We in the modern world can begin to understand something of what Matthew was trying to do in this story by reflecting on the lives and deaths of latter-day heroes like Martin Luther King, Jr., in this country, or Mohandas K. Gandhi in India, or Oscar Romero and Jean Donovan in El Salvador. These people so identified themselves with a message, a cause, that they gave their lives so that the cause would not be compromised. Like Jesus, these people could have decided to stop teaching, to simply go home and pacify those who were against them, thereby removing the threat that was the witness of their lives. Instead, they held fast to their cause until their deaths. For Matthew, Jesus' cause is God, and Jesus' witness to the love of God is made stronger by the fact that he dies horribly rather than succumb to the pressure of his detractors.

American history since the assassination of Martin Luther King, Jr., has demonstrated what a powerful influence his life had on those who believed in racial equality. Indeed, the Civil Rights movement has produced many martyrs who believed that their cause was just. A similar dynamic characterized the early church. The early Christians were so convinced by Jesus' life and death that they were themselves willing to die in witness to the love of God. Matthew, like the other Evangelists, wanted to convey something of this sentiment. For him, Jesus is a hero, but also more than a hero. Jesus' cause is to him *the* cause, God's reaching into human history to be with his beloved people to convince them of his care, to give their lives ultimate meaning. Again and again Matthew shows Jesus teaching about "the kingdom of heaven," to indicate that in the future he will join his followers in the presence of the living God. Jesus is the hero to beat all heroes because he not only speaks of the final meaning of human life but also brings it about through the gift of himself.

Compared to the rest of Matthew's Gospel, the account of Jesus' passion and resurrection is remarkably detailed. Much of the Gospel is choppy, suggesting that Matthew strung together a number of different stories without specific regard for creating a narrative flow. But the end of his Gospel reads like a continuous story, involving not only Jesus but also various leaders and some of his disciples. It is very realistic: Matthew does not attempt to paint a rosy picture of the events. One of his disciples, Judas, betrays him; another, Peter, denies knowing him. People make fun of Jesus left and right. And perhaps most surprisingly, near the end, Jesus cries out to God, asking why he has forgotten about him. Here, in contrast, is a very human reaction of loneliness and fear, which Jesus expresses using the first few words of Psalm 22. The rest of the psalm reads as follows:

> My God, my God, why have you forsaken me?
>> Why are you so far from helping me, from the
>> words of my groaning?
> O my God, I cry by day, but you do not answer;
>> and by night, but find no rest.
>
> Yet you are holy,
>> enthroned on the praises of Israel.
> In you our ancestors trusted;
>> they trusted, and you delivered them.

To you they cried, and were saved;
in you they trusted, and were not put to shame . . .
All who see me mock at me;
they make mouths at me, they shake their heads;
"Commit your cause to the LORD; let him deliver—
let him rescue the one in whom he delights!". . .

they divide my clothes among themselves,
and for my clothing they cast lots.

But you, O LORD, do not be far away!
O my help, come quickly to my aid . . .

I will tell of your name to my brothers and sisters;
in the midst of the congregation I will praise you: . . .
(Psalm 22: 1–5; 7–8; 18–19; 22)

The psalm was for Matthew another prophecy of Jesus, including the reference to the jeers of onlookers and their contest over ownership of his garments. On a deeper level, though, Matthew uses this psalm to suggest that Jesus' response to his own death is characteristic of the faithful person. The cry "Why have you abandoned me?" is not a cry of contempt for God, but one of confusion arising from faith. The latter part of the psalm emphasizes that the speaker will continue to praise God before people, even in the midst of suffering.

Matthew's insight here is rich. Authentic Christian spirituality must confront the problems of suffering and death, and the accompanying doubts about God's mercy and power. A simple response might be similar to one of those offered by the friends of Job in the Old Testament, that perhaps suffering is the result of personal sin or lack of faith. But Jesus, like Job, is a man of faith. And both respond to suffering the way any of us would, with cries of anguish and confusion: How can this happen to me? Jesus' words on the cross remind us that suffering is real, and that, because of it, we can feel abandoned by God. God did not (could not?) keep his only son from a horrible death, and yet Jesus keeps faith. Why? And perhaps more importantly, why ought we to have faith in God when there is so much suffering?

Matthew's story continues as an answer to these questions. The death of Jesus is not the end of the story. Matthew alone among the Evangelists highlights that the authorities take precautions to guard the tomb in order to diffuse any claims about Jesus' Resurrection:

> The next day, that is, after the day of Preparation, the chief priests and the Pharisees gathered before Pilate and said, "Sir, we remember what that impostor said while he was still alive, 'After three days I will rise again.' Therefore command the tomb to be made secure until the third day; otherwise his disciples may go and steal him away, and tell the people, 'He has been raised from the dead,' and the last deception would be worse than the first." (Matthew 27:62–64)

This emphasis serves Matthew's objective of showing that the Resurrection is not a deception, that Jesus, in fact did rise from the dead. Perhaps Matthew was trying to debunk the claims of those who were persecuting the Christians at the time he wrote his Gospel, for again in 28:11–15 he writes (alone among the Evangelists) that the elders paid the guards at the tomb to say that Jesus' body was stolen by the disciples. In any case, Matthew recounts that Jesus really did rise from the dead, and that the Resurrection produced great joy in his followers. Moreover, it is when the resurrected Jesus appears to the disciples in Galilee that he makes profound statements about his role in the order of history:

> And Jesus came and said to them, "All authority in heaven and on earth has been given to me. Go therefore and make disciples of all nations, baptizing them in the name of the Father and of the Son and of the Holy Spirit, and teaching them to obey everything that I have commanded you. And remember, I am with you always, to the end of the age." (Matthew 28:18–20)

Here, then, is a Jesus who is no longer concerned with his past suffering, his past doubts, but one who has full confidence in himself and his message: all will be well for those who follow him.

The Resurrection is the event through which the entire story of Jesus becomes clear, and, indeed, it is the event that makes Jesus' life worth recording. Had the story ended with Jesus' death, it would have been more of a tragedy than truly a source of "good news." For Matthew, as for the other Evangelists, the story of Jesus' life is the source of God's revelation to human beings. As a member of the early Christian community, Matthew was part of a (then) small movement that saw in the life and teaching of Jesus something that gave their lives meaning: hope. Matthew's is a gospel of hope, exemplified in the Sermon on the Mount (see Matthew 5:3–12): the kingdom of heaven belongs to the "poor in spirit" and to those who are persecuted for the sake of what is good. Like any story, this gospel must be judged by its ending, and Matthew hints that all human lives are the same. If the ending is hopeful, then even in spite of the travails of the main characters, the story is a happy one.

For the skeptic, the gospel accounts of the Resurrection are difficult to believe. Few people have difficulty accepting that Jesus was a wise man. But even in the early church, people struggled with the hard-to-accept claim that God raised Jesus from the dead: perhaps he wasn't really dead; perhaps he didn't really rise. Paul, writing some thirty years after the events recorded in the Gospels, responds to these reservations:

> For if the dead are not raised, then Christ has not
> been raised. If Christ has not been raised, your
> faith is futile and you are still in your sins. Then
> those also who have died in Christ have perished.
> If for this life only we have hoped in Christ, we
> are of all people most to be pitied. But in fact
> Christ has been raised from the dead, the first
> fruits of those who have died. . . . Otherwise,
> what will those people do who receive baptism
> on behalf of the dead? If the dead are not raised
> at all, why are people baptized on their behalf?

And why are we putting ourselves in danger every hour? I die every day! That is as certain, brothers and sisters, as my boasting of you—a boast that I make in Christ Jesus our Lord. If with merely human hopes I fought with wild animals at Ephesus, what would I have gained by it? If the dead are not raised,

> "Let us eat and drink,
> for tomorrow we die."
> (1 Corinthians 15:16–20; 29–32)

Consider this paraphrase of Paul's first-century Greek:

I know what you're saying: dead people don't just rise. But this means that the story of Jesus' resurrection is false, and that we're all just as screwed up as before, and that those who died believing in resurrection are just plain dead. So if we actually believe in resurrection, we're the biggest idiots of all. *But*, I'm telling you, Jesus really *did* rise from the dead no matter what you say, and he was only the first. We become Christians because we believe that the same will happen to us. Why else would we become Christians? We put ourselves in danger for doing so. For me, being Christian means facing death every day, but I do it because I have faith. I was almost killed in Ephesus—why did I bother? Without faith, we all might as well just have a good time—live it up now, because we'll all end up dead.

Paul understands that for those who did not see the resurrected Jesus, it is difficult to believe that the Resurrection is true. But he emphasizes that the Resurrection is more than just a kind of magic act. It is proof of God's ultimate care for human beings, for by demonstrating the reality of the Resurrection, Jesus invites people to share in it. Christ is only the "first fruits of those who have died," the one who signals the hope that is available to all people. Paul's conviction is sealed by the fact that he relies on it throughout his life: "I die every day," but he keeps trusting that the gospel is true and that the resurrection hope gives his life meaning. Without this hope, Paul realizes, it would be better to simply enjoy oneself as long as possible: "Let us eat and drink, for tomorrow we die."

Christians today still wrestle with the difficulty of believing in the Resurrection, even as they proclaim it year after year at Easter. Faith, though, involves the persistence of belief, sometimes when one's rationality suggests that it is off the mark. Like Paul, Christians continue to work to proclaim the gospel with the belief, the trust, that it is true. And what continues to surprise these Christians is that they retain the energy to do this in the face of terrific difficulty. Sometimes the work itself, being for others who are ignorant, sick, poor, imprisoned, or unloved, provides the encouragement that enables them to keep believing for at least another day.

The Bible as Prayer

The most fundamental act of prayer is turning to God to speak or listen. To enter into the presence of God, Christians often use texts from the Bible. When they do this, they do more than simply read what the text says. They allow the text to become a reminder of God's love. To use an analogy, when someone receives a letter from a beloved, that person will hold on to the letter, perhaps even carry it around. The letter is a reminder of the beloved, a source of entering into deep, happy memories of time spent with that person. It is valued because it constantly provokes good thoughts, imagination about the future, romantic feelings, and hopeful anticipation of the next meeting. But the letter can also be a source of sadness if the beloved has recently departed for a time or if there is tension in the relationship or if one caused ill feeling in the other because of poorly chosen words. In short, the written text of the letter becomes more than a reminder of stories from a person's life, expressions of love, and good wishes for the other. It becomes the method through which one can, in some sense, "enter" into the presence of the other, even if only through imagination.

For the faithful, the biblical text can be a similar entrance into the presence of God. This entrance is more than imagined, though, even if the imagination is involved. It is real, for the praying person is simply acknowledging the already present God in his or her life. The text can work in different ways: giving the person words with which to praise, thank, or cry out to God; calling to mind the works of God in salvation history; inviting reflection on what God has done for him or her; exhorting the person to act in a new way.

One particular practice of praying with the biblical text is called *lectio divina*, Latin for "sacred reading." Developed in the monastic tradition, the practice of *lectio divina* involves the person's slow, careful reading of the text, dwelling on perhaps one word or phrase like "love" or "mercy" or "wisdom of God." The reader attends to this word, savoring it as if it were a treasured gift from God, allowing all his or her attention to focus on this word. By means of this attention, the person moves into deeper contemplation of the mystery of God, ultimately finding the place where the words fall away and "heart speaks to heart."

Using the Bible as a source of prayer helps us understand our own life as part of the continuing activity of God in human history. People of faith recognize in the stories, prayers, exhortations, reflections, hymns, and laws expressions of themselves: "These words are my words." The biblical text is not just a history; it is a source from which we can draw nourishment for our own spirit. It is about our relationship to God, and the words that help us express our side of the relationship.

Psalm 23: Perhaps the most well-known biblical writing is Psalm 23. One reason for its popularity is that it provides an attractive image with which to picture God: "The Lord is my shepherd." This psalm is a good example of how the Bible can provide words that can help us express our spirituality.

> The LORD is my shepherd, I shall not want.
> He makes me lie down in green pastures;
> he leads me beside still waters;
> he restores my soul.

He leads me in right paths
   for his name's sake.
Even though I walk through the darkest valley,
   I fear no evil;
for you are with me;
   your rod and your staff—
      they comfort me.
You prepare a table before me
   in the presence of my enemies;
you anoint my head with oil;
   my cup overflows.
Surely goodness and mercy shall follow me
   all the days of my life,
and I shall dwell in the house of the LORD
   my whole life long.

There is a certain peacefulness to this psalm, as if the very recitation of the words is soothing. The image of the shepherd, even for those who live in cities, is nonetheless a good one for the ideas of protection and care that it suggests. We can imagine God as a shepherd giving his sheep what they need, protecting them from predators, and seeking them out when they are lost. The other biblical references to the "good shepherd" reinforce this idea.

In the Twenty-third Psalm, God the shepherd leads the sheep to a place where they will thrive: the "green pasture" affords the sheep a place where their physical needs are taken care of, a place where they are allowed to roam freely. The "waters" are safe from those who might harm the sheep. One can imagine that, as the day draws to an end, the shepherd guides the sheep along the way back to where they belong. The shepherd cares for them simply because they are his/hers.

Midway through the psalm, the writer moves away from the imagery of the shepherd and focuses on the notion of care. In the "dark valley," with which every person can identify, God remains by the writer's side, encouraging the writer to press on. In the midst of trouble, God still takes care of the needs of God's beloved. God "anoints" the person, a symbol in ancient Israel which connoted welcome, and perhaps even some kind of preparation for action. Even now, the writer's cup overflows: God has provided a superabundance of goodness, such that the gladness of the guest will never come to an end. With this hopefulness, the writer can be at rest in the place God has prepared, in the very house of God. The writer will be treated as a guest for years to come.

Psalm 23 can be a source of hope, a reflection of thanksgiving, a prayer for protection. Its meaning changes for us as we read it through differing life circumstances. But inasmuch as it is a prayer, it is an expression of spirituality. It gives us the words that help us focus on the God who is in every minute of our lives. It is especially meaningful when we suffer: there is a reassurance that God cares for us in our pain. The psalm unfolds with the suggestion that there is evil around, but that the shepherd is a protector. And even when we encounter evil, the psalm reminds us that it will not have the last word.

The reality of suffering, no matter what kind, is that which most seriously challenges faith. In the modern world, especially, which has seen concentration camps and genocide, gang warfare, the slaughter of children, and the decimation of communities through drug use and AIDS, suffering is all too real. Sometimes even Christians have wrongly offered facile solutions: the suffering isn't really that bad; don't worry, everything will be fine; it's God's will and there's a reason for everything. These kinds of explanations, while simplistic, demonstrate how much we need to believe that good will triumph. We hunger for goodness, for fairness, and we feel wronged when they seem absent. These symptoms of our hunger for God are not insignificant. They challenge us to soberly address the reality of suffering.

The one consistent response to suffering which Christian spirituality offers us is this: we are not alone. The biblical literature, from the Book of Job in the Old Testament to the Book of Revelation in the New Testament, reminds us that suffering is, indeed, a reality of the human condition, one whose origin is mystery. But it also shows us that faith in God, even in the midst of suffering, is good. There are certainly times in our lives when we might cry out with Jesus: "My God, my God, why have you forsaken me?" (Matthew 27:46; cf. Psalm 22:1). But these are only moments in our lives, and do not represent the final reality. The cross of Christ is the ultimate act of solidarity: God accepts the human condition with its suffering, becomes one of us, and suffers with us. Why? Certainly not because the suffering is unreal or because God wants us to suffer in some sadistic way or because he wants to teach us some tricks to overcome it. Rather, God suffers with us because only in that way can God convince us that suffering is not the end. We move from suffering to life in the "house of the Lord": not in any weird sunlight-streaming-from-above, angels-playing-harps sense, but rather in the most human, most real sense. We become who we are, the kind of persons we catch glimpses of throughout our lives, when we accomplish something of which we are proud; or do some completely good, unselfish act; or love another person without even hoping to get anything in return.

Heaven has always been held out as the hope of all who believe in God. Perhaps heaven is the experience of becoming our real selves, the selves who have been injured by suffering. Perhaps this promise of life is that even though suffering takes life from us, life will not be stolen away forever. Perhaps when we "dwell in the house of the Lord" there will be goodness overflowing to the extent that we will be so filled with life that we will satiate our desires and yet always want more. Jesus' words on the cross were his last, but only until he rose again. Even Jesus, God incarnate, was so possessed by suffering at his death that he could see nothing else. But that was not the final chapter. Perhaps the drama of our lives, as St. Paul assures us, is like that of Jesus. The ending of the story determines the character of the narrative, transforming tragedy into comedy. God's promise is that the story ends well.

John 13:1–20: As noted earlier, the practice of imaginative prayer can enable us to appropriate the biblical text at a deeply personal level. The Gospels are full of stories in which we can imagine ourselves taking part, as if we were dear friends of Jesus or witnesses to his miracles. Such prayer can be enormously fruitful, if we allow this imagination to lead us to know Jesus more intimately.

An example is the story of Jesus washing the feet of the disciples.

> [Jesus] got up from the table, took off his outer
> robe, and tied a towel around himself. Then he
> poured water into a basin and began to wash the

disciples' feet and to wipe them with the towel that was tied around him. He came to Simon Peter, who said to him, "Lord, are you going to wash my feet?" Jesus answered, "You do not know now what I am doing, but later you will understand." Peter said to him, "You will never wash my feet." Jesus answered, "Unless I wash you, you have no share with me." Simon Peter said to him, "Lord, not my feet only but also my hands and my head!" Jesus said to him, "One who has bathed does not need to wash, except for the feet, but is entirely clean. And you are clean, though not all of you." For he knew who was to betray him; for this reason he said, "Not all of you are clean." After he had washed their feet, had put on his robe, and had returned to the table, he said to them, "Do you know what I have done to you? You call me Teacher and Lord—and you are right, for that is what I am. So if I, your Lord and Teacher, have washed your feet, you also ought to wash one another's feet. For I have set you an example, that you also should do as I have done to you. Very truly, I tell you, servants are not greater than their master, nor are messengers greater than the one who sent them. If you know these things, you are blessed if you do them." (John 13:4–17)

When I was in college, I was one of several people who decided to do a directed "in-life retreat," which involved daily prayer and reflection on Scripture, guided by a spiritual director. This was one of the readings I was assigned, and I learned much from praying it. During my prayer, I imagined myself first as Jesus, going around washing people's feet. I was reminded of services on Holy Thursday, during which the priest reenacts this action. It struck me as a highly symbolic representation of service. We are called to be of service to others, so this seemed to be good.

I then imagined myself as one of the disciples at the table with Jesus, and found that I had a similar response to that of Peter: "You [Jesus] will never wash my feet." To me it seemed like a sacrilege—Jesus is the Son of God, the person on whom our entire religious belief is based! I simply could not let him do something so menial! In my prayer, I wanted to wash Jesus' feet. It seemed more appropriate.

When I talked to my spiritual director about this prayer, he insightfully asked what this experience told me about my perception of Jesus in my life. I realized that at the time, it meant that my relationship with him was distant: Jesus was the one who was represented on churches, in icons, as the figure on crucifixes, but not one to whom I could reveal my most private thoughts. Jesus was a religious figure, in short, but not a friend. With this insight I began to ponder how the story of the washing of the feet was a kind of "gospel within the Gospel": a symbol of the Christian life. Jesus came to serve us, not as a distant figure but as one who shares our lives, our struggles. In washing feet he demonstrates that he is nowhere near being "above" us; on the contrary, he is, in this action, both literally and figuratively, "below" us, the suffering servant, to use the phrase from the Book of Isaiah. In serving us, Jesus dignifies us. We are worthy enough to have as our servant the Son of God!

A further reflection took hold. I realized that the service to which all Christians are called in imitation of Jesus depends on those we serve. Love is not the isolated action of an individual. Rather, it requires that there be someone who can receive our love. By my refusing Jesus' act of love, I did not even permit him to show how much he loved me. I further understood that I had done this at other times in my life. Ours is a culture of individualism; our theme is "Thanks, but I can handle it." Too often in the name of self-sufficiency we deny each other the opportunity to do something selfless, and as a result we fall out of the practice of trying. It is good to allow others to serve us, to love us, even if in doing so we assume a position of dependence. The one who loves, who serves, is often in the position of power—think of one who gives food to a poor person—and it can be difficult to assume the opposite position of dependence. Yet, such an act of trust can provide the chance for goodness, for love, and where there is love (so goes the hymn) God is there: *Ubi caritas et amor, Deus ibi est.*

This one prayer over a single gospel story led me to a rich understanding. I often remember that experience as I struggle with questions of how to serve and how to let others be of service to me. Now that I am a husband and a father, these questions assume a certain potency. In any close relationship, there is the dynamic of giving and receiving. Indeed, many relationships fail precisely because there is an imbalance between these two actions.

Yet, the practice of giving and receiving is the practice of wisdom. It is the constant vigilance that seeks to understand the people around us, as Jesus did. In many examples he is a giver: healing, teaching, comforting. But in others he is a masterful receiver: he receives from the woman who anoints his feet; he receives from John the Baptist at his baptism; he even receives from a soldier a drink while he's dying on the cross. We tend to more easily identify with the giving side, however: giving involves action, and it is almost always possible to act. But receiving as Jesus did also involves action. For example, communicating my needs is difficult, for it makes me vulnerable, but it provides those I love with opportunities for giving. Accepting another's help, even when I do not need it, is also an act of receiving. Acknowledging the actions of others is also a reception of their loving action.

The love of God for people is no different. The Old Testament can be roughly described as the chronicle of God's giving and of Israel's repeated refusal to receive. Time and again, God promises to love his people and to enter a relationship with them, but just as often, it seems, they forget. The Book of Hosea is a particularly poignant example of this dynamic. God asks the prophet Hosea to marry a prostitute, which he does. Hosea's unfaithful marriage, says God, is like the relationship of God to Israel. He is continually frustrated in his attempts to reach his people. The parable of the landowner in the Gospels echoes this similar theme (see Matthew 21:33–46; Mark 12:1–12; Luke 20:9–19): the landowner sends various servants to collect from the tenants; the tenants kill all the servants; the landowner (God) sends his son, who is also killed by the tenants (humanity). God's love is powerless unless it is received. But when it is received in faith, it produces abundant goodness.

In the case of the story of the washing of the feet, Peter's reception of Jesus' action foreshadows his later role among the apostles. Even in spite of his rejection of Jesus, Peter's proclamation of faith, in this story and elsewhere, provides the foundation for his actions in establishing the Church, as recorded in the Acts of the Apostles. Peter experiences a small conversion in this story, allowing the one he called master to become servant. And Jesus' words to him reinforce the idea that those who would teach in the name of God must also become servants.

These observations are a brief look into why the biblical text is so important for Christians. It gives us the language with which to pray. For those who are interested in learning more about how to pray using different texts in the Bible, I have included an appendix that gives some suggestions (see page 139).

In the next chapter, we explore the importance of Christians praying together, the value of being part of a praying community, a church, and the meaning of "sacrament," the ritual prayer of the Christian community, paying particular attention to the Eucharist (the celebration of Jesus' Last Supper with his disciples) and to sex and marriage as important examples of sacrament.

For Group Discussion

1. What biblical stories were you taught as a child? Were you encouraged to read the Bible for yourself? If so, what did you think about what you read?
2. Who do you think Jesus is?
3. Which biblical texts have particular meaning for you?
4. What do the creation stories tell us about God? How can these stories affect our views, for example, of the environment, human rights, or sex?
5. What strikes you about the story of Jesus' death? Do you see him as similar to other people who have died for what they believe in? What about the story of Jesus is unique?
6. Does the fact that Matthew was Jewish affect your reading of his story about Jesus? Does the fact that another Evangelist, Luke, was Greek make any difference in his story? Do factors like living in the first century C.E. or being male or writing in Greek or hearing the stories secondhand affect how we ought to understand what the Evangelists wrote?

7. What strikes you about Psalm 23? Do you understand it today the same way you might have understood it when you were a child? What does this tell you about your understanding of God?

8. Are you comfortable with the idea of Jesus serving you? Is this idea consistent with the way you view Jesus?

Breaking Bread Together:
Jesus Is the Bread of Life

My soul is satisfied as with a rich feast,
and my mouth praises you with joyful lips.
—PSALM 63:5

"I'm not religious, but I consider myself spiritual." More and more, I encounter students and peers who take this attitude. "Church is boring; people are hypocritical; I don't have the time or interest to practice religion. But I am a spiritual person. I try to learn from my mistakes, I care about people and the world, and I want to grow as a human being." This attitude is laudable in many ways, of course, because it is an acceptance of personal responsibility in the face of the mystery of life. It is not blindly following the ways of everyone else, as some suggest religious people have done in the past. Rather, it takes seriously the ethical demands of living in a complex world.

I want to challenge this attitude, however, by saying that it is fundamentally misdirected—there is no such thing as "personal spirituality" without community responsibility. Certainly in the Christian tradition, spirituality is a public as well as a private endeavor. But an authentic understanding of spirituality takes seriously the idea that it must be grounded in a community.

I am reminded of a commercial that came out a while ago that showed a group of people standing on the shore of the ocean, watching in the distance for the appearance of whales. At a certain point, one of these beautiful creatures came out of the water and made a tremendous splash, leading one of the people to exclaim with great wonder: "This is *so spiritual!*" I forget what product was being advertised, but what stuck in my mind was how that person's comment in that situation represented the leading misunderstanding of spirituality: namely, that it is the feeling of wonder in the face of mystery. We often think that spirituality is about feeling something awesome—that mix of fear and attraction and confusion and wonder. To be sure, spirituality does sometimes involve such feelings; but to believe that this is what spirituality is all about is to mistake the symptom for the cause. Unfortunately, when people don't get this feeling by going to church, they assume that the church is to blame, and they go out to seek their spirituality elsewhere (books, pseudo-religious groups, travels to exotic places, aromatherapy, music).

There certainly is nothing wrong with the feeling I have described, or with seeking experiences that produce it; it can be part of living deeply. But it is wrong to assume that this feeling is what spirituality is about. The fundamental mistake is that these kinds of feelings are self-focused and tend to make us selfish—the constant attempt to get a certain feeling, not unlike a high. Spirituality, however, is not about feeling; it is about encountering God. And while the encounter with God can produce a rush, it often is as ordinary as the business of living. In fact, at times it can be positively depressing. Again, it is much like being in love.

We must practice spirituality in community because community prevents us from allowing our spirituality to become selfish. It grounds us and reminds us that authentic spirituality involves the often unpleasant business of serving others, thus forcing us to grow by pushing us outside of our comfort zones, which would have us think that God will always give us things we enjoy.

Spirituality Is about Community

Five considerations will help us focus on why we must reach beyond ourselves if we wish to develop an authentic spiritual life. The first three, *community, history,* and *liturgy,* point to our personal limitations as individuals. The last two, *Church and the churches* and *praying with the*

Church, focus on the questions that many young people raise when they consider what community spirituality means for them.

Community

The need to be part of a community of believers becomes evident during the ministry of Jesus. The disciples who gather around Jesus recognize that he has the ability to teach with authority on the power and love of God for his people: God is the good shepherd, the one who tends his flock; the expectant father, who eagerly awaits the return of the prodigal son. In choosing to be with Jesus, the disciples choose to be part of a community of believers. At a basic level, they realize that their common interest, listening to Jesus, make them into a community. At a deeper level, however, they probably understand that following Jesus means they share a common commitment to seek God in all things.

The Church is fundamentally a worshiping community because it is the gathering of those who proclaim "Jesus is Lord." It shares with those who listened to the disciples at Pentecost the conviction that Jesus reveals to us God the Father, and it seeks as a community to make that conviction real in everyday life. This is an ideal, one to which Christians must constantly call each other.

In real life, however, this ideal is difficult to realize. The Church seeks the divine God, but it remains a human institution. The dissensions that were already present in the early church have not gone away, and, as a result, there are divisions among Christians about how to fully live the gospel message today. Far from making that message a lie, however, these dissensions emphasize how authentic it is, and how seriously people take the gospel. They also point out why community is an essential element in authentic Christian spirituality, in spite of its limitations. The community of the Church is necessary because it keeps people from creating a belief in Jesus that has no foundation. Because Christians must constantly call one another to the ideals of Jesus' teachings, they remind one another that spirituality is not merely something that comes from the mind of the praying person. It is God who calls us to worship Christ. We cannot allow our spirituality to arise out of our own prejudices, preferences, predilections, and predispositions. It must be the response to the gospel, the "good news" to which Jesus calls us. To see spirituality as something that gives *me* deeper peace or makes *me* more liberated is to make the mistake of selfishness. If we are to practice a spirituality that is not of our own narrow making, we need community.

Many people understand the need for community on a basic level. We want to know that other people share the same questions, the same desire to make sense of things, the same struggles. A friend recounted to me her experience of needing a community when faced with the difficulty of caring for her special-needs child. She described how she needed to know that other parents were able to deal with their children, and how it was possible to go on with life facing this new struggle. Another friend told me how, when he suffered an injury that left him a quadriplegic, he was on the brink of suicide and was basically saved by people who showed him that they, too, had suffered terribly and were still able to build a life after the event. These are extreme examples, but they show how important it is to seek out others when we are faced with deep questions about pain, suffering, life, and death. If Christian faith is about these kinds of ultimate questions, then it cannot be a solitary endeavor.

History

In a similar way, Christian spirituality must be connected to a history that involves the unfolding of God's revelation to people, culminating in the life of Jesus. In our age we have a tendency to think of spirituality as something mystical, otherworldly, mysterious. But Christian spirituality must be grounded in history because, in its essence, it is about the work of being human. Moreover, its development over the centuries has been due, in part, to the work of ordinary human beings who have listened to the call of God. The testimonies of the saints remind us that God calls people to particular work in concrete places at specific times. Similarly, there are Christians around the world today who are feeding the hungry, caring for the sick, visiting prisoners, comforting the dying, and doing hundreds of other kinds of ordinary work in Jesus' name for the glory of God. To "over-spiritualize" Christian spirituality is to forget that God calls us to do things—ordinary and often mundane things—in the usual routine of our daily lives.

Respecting the role of history in the experience of spirituality reminds Christians not to reinvent the wheel. In its two thousand years as a community, the Church has seen every kind of problem we can imagine, thus leaving us today with a wealth of wisdom from which to draw, based on the living reflections of people who have struggled to live faithfully in changing historical circumstances. Those who insist that the Church is beyond help sever the connection with history, and in so doing sever the connection with the community that has, over the centuries, sought diligently to proclaim its belief in Jesus.

Liturgy

Liturgy calls Christians together to share their spirituality in ways that transcend what any individual person can do alone. It is the expression of the already present love of God among the community, the Body of Christ. It crystallizes the spirituality of a church community as a whole, symbolizing its faith. Through liturgy, those of us who struggle in faith find support; those of us who suffer find comfort; those of us who are ignorant discover ways to learn; those of us who have forgotten are helped to remember. Liturgy is important for the Church as Fourth of July parades are important for the country, or as anniversary celebrations are important for a married couple.

These examples are so powerful in the life of a community, and are expressions of a community's history, because they are all symbolic. A *symbol* (from the Greek word meaning "thrown together") is something that gathers into itself a multifaceted, complex reality. A country's flag, for example, calls to mind images of a nation: its history, its key figures, the memories of those who have died defending it, patriotic songs, important celebrations, and a host of other things. As a symbol, a flag is a powerful manifestation of a complex reality.

For Christians, liturgy is a symbol. It can evoke in the worshiping community memories of important events in salvation history, thankfulness for God's care, petitions for God's help, recollections of the love of different people, and hope in heaven. Christians need liturgy the same way all people need the symbols of the things they care about most: wedding rings, high school yearbooks, graduation programs, anniversary cards, trophies, tickets from important events, autographs. Without symbols to remind us of the meaningful events in our lives, we have nothing tangible to embody for us that which is significant.

To outsiders, a certain symbol may seem confusing, even ridiculous, because it seems meaningless or trite. For example, many people wear crosses around their necks or on their ears or pinned to their clothing or tattooed on their bodies. No doubt, those who wear them have their reason for doing so. But the wearing of a cross conveys different messages for different people. A woman may wear a cross to show that she is a member of a religious order of sisters; other persons may wear crosses to show that they reject all religion. This one example highlights how difficult it can be to understand the way a symbol is used, and suggests why traditional Christian practices can seem bewildering to those who do not understand the symbols. Liturgy, as the complex manipulation of symbols and symbolic language, movement, sights, sounds, and smells, is meaningless to those who do not understand the purpose and power of symbol.

Thus, those who would worship with other Christians must be "initiated" into the practice of liturgy, the use of Christian symbolism. To use an analogy, imagine that someone who had never seen a professional football game goes to see the Super Bowl. His first impressions will include wonder, confusion, and interest: Why do the people on the field dress that way and why do they act that way? Why is there so much screaming? What odd music this is! What are people drinking? The only way this person might begin to understand what is going on around him is to make some connection between what he sees and some other personal experience he's had. He would more likely make sense of things, however, if he had a guide who was already familiar with the football scene, who could help him understand all the bizarre behavior inside the stadium.

Similarly, people who see Christian symbolism without understanding the worldview that produces it are confused. Christian "initiation" involves introducing people to symbols. We pray the Our Father because Jesus taught it to us; we kneel because it is a show of reverence; we hold hands to show fellowship; we sing psalms because they are the language of praise to God. Understanding the symbolism opens us to a new world of understanding.

Christian symbolism has developed over a long history, and its richness is appreciated by those who return to the same symbols again and again over the course of their lives. A simple example is the sign of the cross, which is a basic prayer that many Christians utter under varying circumstances. The same short prayer can call to mind many different things: simple praise, gratitude before a meal, the public acknowledgment of one's faith, petition, hopefulness. But the prayer can also be trite and meaningless.

To put it simply, symbols are only as meaningful as we allow them to be. Many people go to church their whole lives and never get anything out of it, while others go every day and are constantly renewed. To manifest meaning, a symbol must be invested with meaning. A ring is a symbol only after a couple gets married; a yearbook is a symbol only for those who have connections to the school. The cross is an immensely powerful symbol for Christians, but for those who do not share faith, it is someone else's symbol. I invest a symbol with meaning for me when I make the symbol my own, when I connect it with something in my own life experience. For many young people, Christian symbols are someone else's symbols—and that is why many find going to church so tedious.

Liturgy has the capacity to be a powerful medium of God's grace, but only if we do something to make the symbolism personally meaningful. There is no easy way to do this, however, because there are, admittedly, so many variables. For example, we must first admit that some liturgy is just badly done. A symbol that calls attention to itself because it is itself a weak symbol cannot further manifest a greater reality. It is like hearing "The Star-Spangled Banner" performed by someone who cannot sing. Liturgy must first be done with care if it is to help us know God.

Second, there are so many symbols within the Christian tradition that people must choose which ones to use and how to use them. I suspect that one of the main reasons many young people avoid going to church is that they find it intensely boring. They have witnessed the use of symbolism that is popular among people of different generations, but find that it does little for them. ("Same old songs, same old words, same old stuff.") It is clear, however, that the practice of worship has changed significantly over the centuries, and so it is a mistake to think that any one liturgical practice is not subject to revision. One obvious example is the fact that we now pray in the assembly with words that are different from the words Jesus used. (Very few people speak Aramaic today.) Moreover, as language develops through history, we find that revisions are necessary even when it seems like we are still using the same language. Most recently, many churches have become accustomed to using a more modern English version of the Lord's Prayer: instead of "hallowed be thy name," they say "may your name be holy" or something similar.

Third, realizing the full richness of liturgy is contingent on things like the type of music used, who is involved in the worship, where people stand or sit, the type of lighting used, the tone of the gathering, and the manner of preaching. All these variables enable people to make liturgy their own, thus connecting them to the outward action of worshiping God to the inward action of self-reflection. Liturgy is about God, but it is also about people, and unless liturgy appeals to people, it won't do much good.

Fourth, liturgy is the practice of faith, and as a practice, it involves a community of people, a history, and an ongoing commitment to do it well. In writing about different practices, the philosopher Alasdair Macintyre makes a distinction between what he calls "internal goods" and "external goods."[1] *Internal goods* are those good things people do to pursue some goal, while *external goods* are benefits people receive from pursuing that goal. For example, if I want to become a good basketball player, I must learn the internal goods of dribbling, shooting, and passing. Ultimately, I may gain some external goods, like a scholarship to college, a professional career, perhaps even fame. The practice of faith in liturgy, too, involves both internal goods and external goods. Sometimes the external goods are enough: I may enjoy meeting people, listening to the music, having some time to myself. But ultimately, liturgy must be about the internal good of expressing and sharing faith. In other words, I must practice liturgy not merely as a spectator, but as one who is bringing faith into practice. To be sure, going to church can itself be an act of faith. Even if one is unsure whether worship is useful, the very act of doing it anyway leaves open the opportunity that one will encounter God in a new way.

Personally, I go to church regularly, and have done so my entire life. I say this not to brag but to point out that I have done it long enough to see a lot of things. For example, I've seen the way many people have that far-off look (and I've had it myself), which means the person is there but the mind is wandering. I've seen people looking around the room at other people, at the artwork, at the lights, trying to find some way to pass the time while so-and-so up there on the altar babbles on and on. I've seen the way people wince at the idea of having to sing, how they creep into the back row, hoping not to be seen by anyone else, how they leave early, as if to say, "I've done my duty, but I have to get out of here and watch some football!"

Let's face it: church can be a chore. Just because I continue to go regularly doesn't mean I have some twisted perspective on what's fun and what's not. But I keep going because I believe that God can surprise me. I've had experiences of trudging off to Sunday Mass and merely going through the motions, when something strikes me—a reading, a song, something a person says— and suddenly I find myself wondering if God is trying to get my attention. I am convinced that some of the most important moments in my spiritual life are ones that I could not have planned, but could only have chosen to receive or ignore. For me, being part of Church is a way of being ready to receive what God wants to give me. This all makes sense: if God is free, then we can't plan our spiritual lives according to some schedule. We have to allow God to act when God judges us ready.

Being an active, consistent part of the Church is a regular reminder to ourselves to allow God to act. On a practical level, this means that if we are to practice authentic Christian spirituality, we must find a means of expressing it in a community: a small prayer group, a Bible study, a student gathering. Only in this way can we begin to understand the dynamic between personal faith and community worship, and thus begin to appreciate what it means to be a part of the Church. Hopefully, greater familiarity with liturgy will lead to a greater ease in understanding the symbolism that is shared by Christians at home, across the country, and around the world.

The Church and the Churches

There are literally hundreds of different "churches" in the world today. We can speak of the differences among the Catholic, Orthodox, Lutheran, Baptist, Episcopalian, Methodist, Nazarene, Assemblies of God, and other *churches*, recognizing that there are differing points of doctrine, theology, liturgy, history, *et cetera*. It would be impossible to relate all these differences in a single book, let alone do justice to them in this brief treatment. I distinguish "the Church" (big C) from "the churches" (small c), suggesting that from the perspective of Christian spirituality it is more fruitful to deal with the similarities between Christians of different churches within the Church than to deal with the differences between churches.[2] To be sure, the proclamation "Jesus is Lord" is a statement of faith that Christians of all churches within the Church hold as truth. Thus it is possible, although difficult, to speak of the Church as that group of people who profess this faith and attempt to understand it in their everyday lives within different churches.

The Church is an important part of any Christian spirituality. Fifth-century theologian Prosper of Aquitaine used a phrase that has come to represent this truth for us today: "The law of worship founds the law of belief." In other words, what the Church does when it worships Jesus Christ is what enables Christians to authentically proclaim their beliefs about Jesus. Beliefs *about* Jesus arise out of prayer *to* Jesus, and prayer to Jesus must take place within the community of Christians.

Praying with the Church

To pray with the Church is to become part of a community with a shared history that celebrates its faith in liturgy. Fundamentally, then, praying with the Church is about joining a group of people who, as a church, joins the universal Church in its liturgical celebrations. This simple fact is both obvious and easily overlooked. Sadly, it is often overlooked by churchgoers themselves—those who are in the long-established habit of frequent churchgoing but who sometimes forget that there are those who must be welcomed, encouraged, and invited. Many see the habit of churchgoing as a duty to be fulfilled rather than an opportunity to be seized. As a result, these people tend to focus more on the discharging of duty rather than on the need to construct a community of faith.

Those who are on the "outside"—that is, those who don't feel themselves to be part of the community (this may include people who have been going to the same church for years)—recognize, however, that churchgoing is about people. They understand that there is a group of people who engage in those rituals for whatever reason, and are aware that they are not part of that group. Nevertheless, God calls people to the Church in so many ways, and so the community is constantly renewed. The very desire to try Christian worship is itself a manifestation of the seed of faith, the invitation of God.

Those who try praying with the Church will encounter different kinds of communities in different churches, even in different parishes of the same Christian denomination. Experience convinces many Christians that finding the "right church" is a matter of finding the right community of people, and on one level this is true. Because the Church is the community of those who worship God in the name of Jesus the Christ, "the right church" must involve some level of sharing among members of the local community. But on another level, the Church is the entire people of God. In traditional terminology, it is the "communion of saints" to which the ancient Apostles' Creed makes reference. It is the gathering of all those who have responded to the invitation of God, those who are living and those who have died, all seeking intimacy with God. Thus, the local church is but one part of this communion, and so we ought not to expect that within any single local community we will find the fullness of what it means to be a Christian.

To be more specific, we must face up to our own human limitations in thinking about what the community ought to be. Often, we seek to engage in relationships with other people who are basically similar to ourselves: similar in their economic situation, race, age, and geographic location. While this is not always true, it does suggest that we must be careful not to expect that we will find in a church assembly people exactly like ourselves. On the contrary, perhaps the single greatest challenge the Church has faced over its history is that of trying to reconcile the differences among people who come together as a local or even global community, overcoming differences so that all might be welcome.

While it is important to find a community with whom we can pray, we must not expect to find a church strictly in our own image. Part of what makes the Church unique is that it encompasses all groups of people: young, old, rich, poor, male, female, white, black, brown, Eastern, Western, left-handed and right-handed people. It is not a fashionable organization because it needs to appeal to everyone, not just a limited few. It does not respond to every change that happens in places, because its vision is more farsighted.

One of the most common criticisms among young people, in particular, is that the Church needs to get with the times.[3] And while this is true to some extent, and certainly something with which many Christians wrestle, being modern cannot be the primary focus of the Church's energy—if by "modern" we mean changing in every way that culture changes. The simple fact is that the Church must balance the weight of its history and its gospel message with the changes in contemporary society, and often the proposals of modern culture conflict with the gospel.

Praying with the Church sometimes means being countercultural. It is evident in the New Testament that the early disciples faced this tension, and it is equally evident today. For young people, especially, this tension presents a serious consideration. Young adulthood is characterized by the attempt to insert ourselves into a culture, to find a place. In a culture that extols individualism, achievement, power, attractiveness, and convenience, it seems counterintuitive to practice selflessness, humility, love, and gratitude. Yet, Christian tradition holds that these virtues are more lasting and, in the big picture, more satisfying to the desires of the human heart.

The tension between Church and culture, however, does not always mean that the two are at odds. Many Christians today are important participants in modern culture. Praying with the Church does not mean that we must abandon the world altogether. However, it does mean that, as Christians, we will turn a critical eye toward culture in order to judge the ways in which popular practices affirm or deny the goodness of the individual person before God. It means that we will not blindly assume that majority opinion creates goodness, or that what is new and appealing is automatically worth doing. This tension does sometimes become conflict, as in the examples of certain moral issues upon which the Church has taken a strong stand. But more often, it is a subtle questioning, a seeking to understand life, a living in the horizon of our fundamental stance before the God who loves us eternally.

One example will show how Christians must sometimes challenge the culture's conventional wisdom. A theme that runs through the biblical text is the value and use of money. Where many in this country say "The one who dies with the most toys wins," Christians must face up to the challenge to share their own gifts with others. In this case, Jesus' observation that people can't serve two masters—God and money (see Matthew 6:24; Luke 16:13)—leads many to make choices very different from what the culture promotes. At least with this example, though, Christianity and culture can co-exist peacefully—it is certainly not against the laws of culture to give away money. But it does nonetheless present us with a challenge, particularly if we see our peers getting rich while we struggle to be faithful by not choosing to accumulate wealth. I have friends who have made very difficult choices in response to their faith—a doctor who could make a mint but chooses, instead, to work with low-income people; a couple who, instead of working in the corporate world, spent two years in the Peace Corps and have worked with refugees; a young woman who has spent her early adult life working in various homes for the poor and underprivileged; a woman who left a high-paying job in a major bank to do ministry to teens.

Christian Spirituality Is about Christ and the Church

At the heart of Christian spirituality is Jesus' invitation, "Come, follow me." This invitation, first issued to the disciples, can be seen as a kind of appeal to our curiosity. Why should I follow you? Can't you see I'm kind of busy right now? Surprisingly, the Gospels record little of the disciples' motivation. In some cases, they just drop what they are doing and literally start following Jesus.

Today, it is unlikely that many of us will agree to such an interruption of our lives simply to satisfy curiosity. Yet, this same "curiosity factor" is fundamentally what draws many people to follow Christ, or at least to further question what he is all about. Some are drawn by an experience of liturgy, which they seek to understand further. Others are drawn by a key figure in their lives—a priest, nun, or minister; a religious relative or friend; a famous person like Mother Teresa or Billy Graham or the pope or Bishop Desmond Tutu. In any case, this curiosity draws people to ask questions and to seek answers, similar to the early disciples. What is important to recognize, though, is that it is the Church that draws people to Christ, because it is fundamentally the Church that has, over time, preserved the living memory of Christ.

The prophet Jeremiah lamented that God had "duped" or "seduced" him into his life as a prophet (see Jeremiah 20:7), that, as a prophet, he was compelled to speak the words of God, even to the point of derision by his friends. It is interesting to note that Jeremiah evidently had been *enticed* and perhaps even *tricked* into his role as a prophet, yet he grew so fully into his role that failure to speak for God made his heart burn (see 20:9). Here is one whose "curiosity factor" had drawn him in to the point that he sacrificed everything to be a prophet of God. Similarly, after Peter had been with Jesus for some time, he reflected that there was nothing else he could do: "Lord, to whom can we go? You have the words of eternal life" (John 6:68). Peter had become so thoroughly convinced that Jesus' teaching was right and that Jesus revealed to him the truth of God.

Today, people experience the same kind of conviction about Jesus' life and teaching: it manifests the wisdom of God in unparalleled ways. Over the centuries, the Church has come to understand Jesus' role in history as an absolutely unique one, for only Jesus was "the Christ," the one anointed by God to be present to his people. In theological language, Christ is the "sacrament" of God, the living presence of God's love for people. In Christ, people are moved to the same kind of fundamental conviction shared by Jeremiah and Peter: God alone is the author of truth and life, to the extent that apart from God's truth there is nothing.

Christ as Sacrament

In the person of Christ, God's presence to people takes on a new dimension. In his first letter to Timothy, Paul says that Christ is the "one mediator between God and humankind" (2:5). Christ is not only one who speaks the truth of God; he is not only one whose life testifies to the compassion of God; he is not only one who offers us the hope of final union with God. He is, to use the words of the ancient Nicene Creed, "God from God, light from light, true God from true God, begotten, not made, one in being with the Father." Christ is the incarnation of God, God-become-human, so that the human being might become more like God. We use the ancient Latin term *sacrament* to connote this complex reality of God reaching out to human beings in concrete, human ways.

There is a story that represents something of the truth of the Incarnation, and thus a better understanding of the term *sacrament*. A farmer lamented that he could no longer believe in Christ because he could not believe that God would permit so much suffering in the world. He prayed that he might be restored to faith, and God listened to his prayer. One night during a terrible storm, the farmer noticed that there was a flock of geese running around frightened and unable to protect themselves from the hail and wind. Being of good heart, the farmer ran out to open the door of his spacious barn, intending to provide the geese with a place to rest. But the geese were only more frightened of the farmer, whose attempts to usher them into the barn made them move farther away. The farmer said to himself, "If only I could, for a time, become a goose and lead them into my barn, then they would be safe." It was with this realization that he understood what Christ had done: he had become like us so that he might lead us to safety.

In the centuries following the death of Christ, Christians reflected upon who he was and what he did. The earliest writings about Jesus to which we have access are the letters of Paul, composed during his various travels around the ancient Near East roughly between 45 and 65 C.E. Because these accounts were written only one generation after Jesus' death, they give us a good picture of the development of Christian belief. It is clear that there developed certain statements of belief around Jesus, statements of basic affirmation of him as the Messiah of God, the one who was promised by the Old Testament prophets, the one who had come to save the world. An example is the so-called Philippians hymn, included in Paul's letter to the church at Philippi (c. 59 C.E.) but probably an even earlier hymn about Jesus:

Let the same mind be in you that was in Christ Jesus,
who, though he was in the form of God,
did not regard equality with God
as something to be exploited,
but emptied himself,
taking the form of a slave,
being born in human likeness.
And being found in human form,
he humbled himself
and became obedient to the point of death—
even death on a cross.

Therefore God also highly exalted him
and gave him the name
that is above every name,
so that at the name of Jesus
every knee should bend,
in heaven and on earth and under the earth,
and every tongue should confess
that Jesus Christ is Lord,
to the glory of God the Father
(Philippians 2:5–11).

This rather complex theological statement about Jesus includes a great deal of what the early church struggled to understand about Jesus. There were so many questions: How could Jesus be equal with God? How could God be with us on earth and still be in heaven? How could the eternal God be a temporal human being? Was God a spirit in a human body? Did Jesus just appear human, although he was really divine? Why didn't God choose to be more powerful and make people believe in him? These and other questions were especially difficult in light of the particularly scandalous death Jesus had suffered at the hands of his enemies.

Writings such as the Philippians hymn indicate that the early Christians addressed these questions head-on, not attempting to gloss over an uneasy part of the story of Jesus. Indeed, the Gospels themselves go into excruciating detail of the passion story, chronicling the kinds of suffering and humiliation Jesus endured. Far from trying to hide the embarrassing beginning of the Christian movement (originally called "The Way"), the disciples of Jesus highlighted that they, like Jesus, were persecuted, and that it was precisely through this persecution that God had shown himself to the world. He had come to show compassion (Latin *cum-patio*, literally "to suffer with" us).

This realization took form in the Christian world over time, but by no means was it a seamless development. To be sure, the world of first-century Christianity was not without factions. For example, there were churches in various cities and towns, each with conservative and liberal lines, much as we find today. What is fascinating, however, is that the Church as a whole learned to live with pluralism, even as various Christians sought to eliminate it entirely. Although there were attempts by later figures to create a single, unified account of the Jesus story, there remained in circulation different accounts by Matthew, Mark, Luke, John, and, later, others. These different accounts certainly shared things in common, but there are nonetheless significant departures that led readers to distinct understandings of who Jesus was.

The significance of this historical development of the Church is that Christians of all times have had to struggle with pluralism. Fundamentally, this means that in trying to understand what the Bible says, we must have a measure of humility. My understanding of Scripture may be different from yours, but that does not make me a good person and you a bad person; that does not make me right and you wrong. Instead of focusing on the "right" reading of Scripture, we must be concerned with a "responsible" reading[4]—one that does justice to the text and its history, as well as to the readers and their respective histories. Again, it is important to remember that the development of belief in Jesus took place within the community of the Church, and if we are to practice a spirituality that is based in belief in Christ, we must look to the Church's profession of belief in him. The following points emphasize the characteristics of Jesus and the impact he has had on people's lives, thus helping us better appreciate why Christians look to Jesus as the model for authentic spirituality.

Jesus has a unique understanding about the kingdom of God. His parables, his teachings, his Sermon on the Mount all point to his ministry being one of convincing people that God's kingdom is real, and that people's lives are intimately connected with the development of God's will. It is interesting to note, however, that there is a tension between the kingdom already being established and the kingdom being something in the future. This "already but not yet" tension serves to exhort the Christian to act with faith, hope, and love in all things. Further, it is clear that a hallmark of Jesus' preaching about the kingdom is based on the Father's forgiveness of sins. In other words, Jesus' invitation is to *all people*—a point that cannot be overemphasized.

Today, as then, we recognize divisions along political and religious lines, but Jesus ignores them. He dines with people of different political backgrounds; he dismisses religious laws that prove a hindrance to real compassion; he forgives those who do wrong; he heals those who are not well. He extends his hand to all who will receive it. For us, this means that genuine spirituality is the reaching out, like Jesus, to everyone, especially to those who challenge our comfort zones. Most people of Gen2K have a certain awareness of this idea; we have seen the ugliness of racism, sexism, and homophobia, and can understand the exhortation to treat all people as people.

Jesus' teaching about the kingdom is not soft. It is not merely a come-as-you-are party, suggesting that everyone is the same. Along with his invitation to all people there are his statements about God's separating sheep from goats, wheat from chaff, sinners from righteous. God comes to call sinners (this means everyone), but he calls them as human beings who need to change their ways in order to enter into relationship with God. His is what today would be called "tough love," that ability to love others into recognizing their self-destructive attitudes and behaviors, and helping them change for the sake of that love. Jesus wants everyone to be with him, but he does not want everyone to remain the same. Those who would follow Jesus are forced to make hard choices: to enter the kingdom, to respond to the invitation of Jesus, is to realize that in doing so, we agree to put false selves behind, releasing the tendencies to selfishness. So while Jesus issues the invitation to all people, he also recognizes that not all people are able to respond to it—hence his more enigmatic statements such as "I have not come to bring peace, but a sword" (Matthew 10:34).

For people today, Jesus' invitation is no less real. Jesus invites all people to fall in love with God the way God has fallen in love with us. But like real human love, God's love for us sees us as we can be, even if the sufferings of our lives hinder us from being such perfect people. To respond to the love of God is to understand ourselves as *radically good*, even if outwardly imperfect. It is to believe that we are the creation of God, more precious than anything, and that God's love for us will ensure that even in our brokenness we are never simply tossed aside. Like an artisan, God takes all his broken creations and makes them new again.

This idea can be enormously difficult to understand and live. To confront our false selves means seeing the ways we put on masks and cover the deeper parts of ourselves—and in a fast-paced society, where image is everything, this is especially challenging. Young people everywhere need to establish identities, and so many take their cues from pop culture—we must be beautiful and sexy and smart and hip. We must have the latest cell phones and laptops, wear the latest clothes, listen to the latest music, see the coolest shows and movies. But in God's kingdom, we are told, image is nothing. True, no one wants to be the weird person out of touch with the world—but do we really want to find our fulfillment as human beings in these things? When we confront the mysteries of life and death, joy and suffering, love and evil, do these image enhancers mean anything at all?

Ultimately, our concern with image is about wanting to feel at home with other people—and if this is true, then there is a spiritual dimension even to these desires. But we can too easily lose sight of what's important: not the image but the person, the child of God, who uses the image in order to be a part of the world.

Jesus issues a call to conversion, a "change of heart." The notion of conversion is described by the words of the Old Testament prophet Ezekiel:

> Thus says the Lord GOD: I will give them one
> heart, and put a new spirit within them; I will
> remove the heart of stone from their flesh and
> give them a heart of flesh, so that they may fol-
> low my statutes and keep my ordinances and

> obey them. Then they shall be my people, and I
> will be their God (Ezekiel 11:17, 19–20).

Conversion in the biblical sense means allowing God to recreate our very selves anew, to remove all that has bound us so that we might again be free. It recognizes that over the course of our lives, there are choices that determine what kind of persons we become, and that sometimes our choices lead us away from God. Jesus' call to conversion is the invitation to respond to God's forgiveness, the opportunity to renew the relationship without the hindrance of old faults. It is important to recognize that it is God who calls us first. Like the father in the story of the prodigal son, God eagerly awaits the return of his beloved.

Conversion is part of ordinary life, to the extent that it involves changing ourselves when we realize our faults. On a spiritual level, though, conversion means always letting God change the way we think about God. When I was a child, I used to think God was "up in the sky"; now I understand that this sense of "where" God is can't be true. I have undergone a kind of conversion, even without being able to put my finger on when it happened.

Some conversions are memorable: "I once was lost, but now I'm found," goes the hymn "Amazing Grace." But more often our conversions are subtle, and we may not even be aware of them except in retrospect.

The experience of conversion means that we are willing to name our faults rather than simply ignoring them. We are able to admit that our behavior often hurts ourselves and others—and that we are willing to change. The good news is that throughout the Gospels, Jesus constantly reaches out to help people toward conversion. The people to whom he acts most harshly are those who are too stuck in their ways to realize the freedom of conversion—the Pharisees, the self-righteous, the arrogant, the egocentric; in effect, those who are too proud to allow Jesus help them.

It saddens me that churches often come across as condemning rather than forgiving those who sin. In my experience with young adult ministry, many people are ashamed to come back to church because they are troubled by something in their past that they see as unforgivable. What we see in Jesus is a person who forgives anyone who is willing to receive it. This is harder than it sounds, of course! It is not simply pretending that our mistakes in the past never happened; rather, it is recognizing the ways that we have caused pain, but choosing to be the kind of person who will not behave that way again. Conversion is, in this sense, becoming a new person: hence the language of being "born again," common among many Evangelical Christians. The basic idea is right: when we undergo conversion, even on a subtle level, we allow God to recreate us anew.

Jesus' actions reinforce what he teaches. His reaching out to the sick, the lonely, the despised, the rejected people of his world emphasize that his ministry is not about praising good people as much as it is about healing, both physically and spiritually. Again and again he uses stories and actions to show that God wants to love people, and wants people to love him in return. The story of the ten lepers is an example.

> On the way to Jerusalem Jesus was going through the region between Samaria and Galilee. As he entered a village, ten lepers approached him. Keeping their distance, they called out, saying, "Jesus, Master, have mercy on us!" When he saw them, he said to them, "Go and show yourselves to the priest." And as they went, they were made clean. Then one of them, when he saw that he was healed, turned back, praising God with a loud voice. He prostrated himself at Jesus' feet and thanked him. And he was a Samaritan. Then Jesus asked, "Were not ten made clean? But the other nine, where are they? Was none of them found to return and give praise to God except this foreigner?" (Luke 17:11–18)

In this story, Jesus heals the lepers out of compassion, but shows genuine hurt that only one returns to give thanks to God. As in other stories, the Samaritan represents the group of people despised by Jesus' contemporaries, yet only he does what God desires. Jesus shows us the difficulty of one-sided love: seeking the good of the other without the reciprocation of that love. In this way, the story is an example of God's relationship to people. God wants our good, but too often we do not respond to God's presence in our lives.

It is important to practice thankfulness in a culture that encourages us to want more and more. True, our economy is based on "wanting"; but our spiritual lives are based on being thankful for the sheer gift of existence. The old habit of saying grace before meals is an example of the virtue of thankfulness—it's a way of reminding ourselves not to take so much for granted. In the Gospels, Jesus is always acknowledging God the Father—his daily life is imbued with the awareness of the Father's presence. How often do we give any thought to God?

The abundance of writings about Jesus testify to his impact on people's lives. Without these writings, i.e., without the faithful followers of Jesus (the Church), there would be no Christian faith. In other words, we come to know Jesus through the Church, both in its history and in the community of people who still hold the Bible to be the Word of God.

The Church is, in a basic sense, that community which says, "Read this and meet Jesus!" It was the early church that sought to understand who Jesus was and why he did what he did, and, most importantly, why he had to die the way that he did. Writings about Jesus were circulated as early as a generation after he died—this fact is extraordinary, considering how few literate people there were in the world at the time. Clearly, the fact that there developed so many writings within a century after Jesus' death and resurrection points to the kind of conviction he produced in those who followed him, and in the ability of the first disciples to produce a similar conviction in those who followed them.

As the Church grew in the years following Jesus' death and resurrection, however, people raised more and more difficult questions. By the time the Gospels were written, no doubt most of the people who had actually seen Jesus were dead. Without these "first-generation" Christians, later believers were left to speculate about what Jesus was like, based on the stories they had received. It is clear that there arose disputes over who Jesus really was, disputes that remained in different forms throughout Christian history, even into modern day.

What is important is that the Church ultimately recognized Jesus as the very incarnation of God, fully God but fully human at the same time. Jesus was God, but not so distant that he doesn't hear us. Jesus was a person who suffered, felt rejected, had friends, scraped his elbow, got hungry, and sometimes needed a break.

Over the centuries, the Christian understanding of Christ enabled theologians to adapt their teachings to different communities, so that they might help people understand a Jesus who was relevant to their own lives. Today, the same challenge exists. To say that Jesus was both divine and human is to make strong claims. Jesus offers God's forgiveness of our sins, wanting to show God's powerful love for us. He shows us what God's world is like, and how God invites us to take our place in it. He reconciles people who have only shared hatred. He sends his Spirit to be with us, to guide us away from self-destructive choices toward choices that are loving. He comforts us in our despair, and reminds us gently that our lives are always meaningful because we are the good creations of God.

But Jesus is not only some distant, disembodied spirit who cannot understand what we are going through. He was a person who had to listen to his parents when he didn't want to; who felt awkward while he was growing up; who experienced sexual attractions; who listened to his friends' problems and shared their distresses; who struggled with questions about what to do with his life. Like the rest of us, Jesus had to confront his problems and rely on the Father.

Christ is the sacrament of God, the person in whom God has become physically present to people. As the Church grew, it came to an understanding of itself as continuing Christ's ministry to people, being Christ for the world. Its aspirations are the same today.

Church as Sacrament

The understanding of the Church as a sacrament of God is based historically on Jesus' promises to his followers: "I am with you always, to the end of the age" (Matthew 28:20). "Peace be with you. As the Father has sent me, so I send you" (John 20:21). The Church does what Jesus did, acting as the physical, tangible, historical presence of God to people. To be a Christian, a follower of Christ, is to (try to) be like Jesus. It is to love others as Christ loves, to be present to people the way God wants to be present to people. For this reason, the Church has always sought to act with mercy toward those who need it most.

Feeding the hungry, caring for the sick, clothing the naked, visiting the abandoned are all examples of this ministry. Authentic Christian spirituality is based in love: the two great commandments—love of God and love of neighbor—recognize this truth. Indeed, the two are inseparable.

Unfortunately, however, the most overused and misunderstood word in the English language is *love*. Look at how we use the same term to refer to our feelings for just about everything: our favorite food, weekends, cars, friends, family, romantic interests, and God! The distinguishing characteristic of Christian love, however, is that it is precisely *not* a feeling or an emotion. Were it a kind of feeling, the commandment "love your enemy" could make little sense—How can I suddenly feel warm toward someone who has hurt me? Instead, Christian love (*agape* in the Greek New Testament) refers to action that arises out of our concern for the good of another. It is possible, then, to love another person even if we cannot stand being with that person.

A good example of this kind of love is portrayed in the movie *The Perfect Storm*. There's a scene in which two men who can't stand each other are out on a fishing boat at night, miles from land. One is cursing out the other, when all of a sudden his hand gets caught in the line and he goes sailing into the cold, dark sea. The other man immediately dives into the water and saves the guy. The next day, the character who almost died grudgingly goes to thank the man who saved him—the one he hated so much. The feeling in the scene is uncomfortable; neither man likes the other, and yet both know that one has done something heroic for the other.

The commandments of love go beyond orders to feel nice. They demand the restraint of destructive tendencies, such as hatred, rancor, revenge; and the practice of constructive tendencies, such as giving and forgiving. Why? Because through the exercise of these constructive tendencies, we become more fully human, and develop the habits that better enable us to know God. People who are able to *love* even those they do not *like* have a better sense of themselves; they seem to have more control over themselves because they do not fall prey to anger or resentfulness. They realize how negative emotions hinder them from being the kind of people they choose to be, and seek to overcome them through the practice of love.

The Church is the sacrament of God insofar as it is the community of people who love as Jesus loved. It is the community that seeks to be God's hands, eyes, ears, muscles, and hugs to people in need—and everyone is needy. Indeed, the Church is not a perfect community, but it constantly tries to reinvent itself in ways that will foster this fundamental goal of loving.

In his great work *The Brothers Karamazov*, Russian writer Fyodor Dostoevsky describes a scene in which the saintly Fr. Zossima responds to a woman who asks how she can regain her lost faith in God. He responds:

> By the experience of active love, strive to love your neighbor actively and indefatigably. In as far as you advance in love you will grow surer of the reality of God and of the immortality of your soul. If you attain to perfect self-forgetfulness in the love of your neighbor, then you will believe without doubt, and no doubt can possibly enter your soul. This has been tried. This is certain.

When the woman responds by talking of her difficulty in loving, Fr. Zossima clarifies what he means. It is an insightful look into what Christian *agape* love is about:

> Love in dreams is greedy for immediate action, rapidly performed and in the sight of all. Men will even give their lives if only the ordeal does not last long but is soon over, with all looking on and applauding as though on the stage. But active love is labor and fortitude, and for some people too, perhaps, a complete science. But I predict that just when you see with horror that in spite of all your efforts you are getting further from your goal instead of nearer to it—at that very moment I predict that you will reach it and behold clearly the miraculous power of the Lord

who has been all the time loving and mysteriously
guiding you.[5]

Too often we love selfishly—that is, we love for some benefit we realize, perhaps a sense of purpose, nobility, or even a sense of self-sacrifice.
To love another can be an egocentric exercise. This is often the case with
romantic love, when what is actually happening is that we are *loving the
feeling* of being in love. But even in the love that does not involve
attraction—the love we experience for family, friends, and even
strangers—we sometimes are hiding ulterior motives. To love as Christ
loves means to love for the greater glory of God, not for the greater
glory of ourselves.

Celebrating Sacraments

There are many ways in which the Church manifests God's love for
people. By simply gathering together, people love. Praying together,
especially, demonstrates a level of trust that is often overlooked in
ordinary worship. Christians show God's love when they visit the sick,
reach out to the lonely, bring food to families who are hungry, listen to
their friends' problems, help neighbors move into their new home, or
simply give hugs to their spouses. In other words, any act of kindness
becomes sacramental when it exemplifies God's love for people.

The most powerful examples of this love, however, are those that
are celebrated by the whole Christian community as explicit manifes-
tations of Christ's love for people. Such acts of love find their origin in
the ministry of Jesus and are carried on by the Church as both a
remembrance and a celebration of Jesus' continuing care.

Baptism is such a sacrament. It recalls the work of John the Baptist,
and particularly the baptism of Jesus. It celebrates God's offer of forgiveness of sin and continues the work that Jesus directed his apostles
to undertake. Most fundamentally, baptism represents God's love for
people. In baptism, we are called into the communion of the Church,
invited to participate in that community which responds to God's
desire to love. Baptism celebrates our turning away from sin, that
which prevents us from living as we are created to live.

But how does baptism "work"? After all, there are many who have been baptized as infants and who have never sought to live holy lives or even go to church. What is the point of baptism if it seems to "work" only some of the time? And how can it, then, manifest the love of God for people?

The answer to these questions points to another fundamental truth of Christian spirituality: God does not force us into anything. A life in the Spirit never involves our having to do that which we do not ourselves choose. Stating it another way, we ourselves choose how much we want to love God, and, as a consequence, we ourselves choose how much we want God to direct our lives. The medieval theologians gave expression to this understanding of the sacraments in this way. Sacraments involve both the grace of God, which God always extends to people; and the action of people who sometimes receive that grace but other times do not. In other words, God's grace is the gift, but we must unwrap it. Grace is the listener, but we must speak. Grace is the speaker, but we must listen. Grace is the lover, but we must choose to love back.

Baptism, then, like the other sacraments of the Church, is an event of both God's grace and our response. Through baptism, we are invited into the Church; but over time we may choose either to celebrate that truth or reject it. Baptism itself guarantees nothing but God's continued love for us through the ministry of the Church. It cannot guarantee that we receive that love or seek to return it. God made us free persons, and our freedom means that we can choose to love—or not. Thus, all who are part of the Church are baptized, but not all who are baptized choose to be part of the Church.

The importance of baptism is similar to the importance of wedding vows. It represents a particular moment in our ongoing relationship with God, an especially powerful moment. Baptism is the response to God's specific invitation to be part of the Church. It is a recognition of Christ's role in the divine plan, a response to God's call to believe in the good news that God has come to be with us in the person of Jesus. It is a call to an intimacy with God through the work of the Holy Spirit, who moves us to know Jesus Christ as the one sent by the Father to call us personally. Baptism then, is *our* response to this invitation. To ignore it by rationalizing that "in the big picture, baptism is not necessary" is like arguing to our beloved, "I'm not going to marry you, because in the big picture, marriage is not necessary." We who are called into baptism ought to be baptized simply because God loves us and wants our love in return.

What does this mean for those who were baptized as infants, who made no choice of their own? Simply this: God has already called them, and today is a good time to celebrate God's love.

The Eucharist

Eucharist is another sacrament of the Church, the celebration of the Lord's Supper. The word *eucharist* comes from the New Testament Greek word which means "thanksgiving," and refers both to Jesus' action of giving thanks at the Last Supper and to the Church's practice of breaking bread together after Jesus' resurrection and ascension. In the celebration of the Eucharist, we find perhaps the most obvious symbolic action: sharing a meal, a banquet. For many Christians, the sharing of the Eucharist is the sacrament that most clearly demonstrates the wisdom of Christian spirituality. Its meaning is on many levels. Most basically, it involves the sharing of food and all that feasting together represents: the satiating of hunger, the joy of company, the sharing of memories and hopes, the resolution of disagreements. It also involves the recollection of Jesus' ministry, particularly the Last Supper. On a deeper level, it refers to Jesus' words "This is my body" and "This is the cup of my blood," words that Christians of all times, like the disciples, struggle to understand. It points to the cross and resurrection of Jesus, the core events that form the central mysteries of the Christian faith.

In John's Gospel, Jesus makes the striking statement, "I am the bread of life. Whoever comes to me will never be hungry, and whoever believes in me will never be thirsty" (6:35). The metaphor here is clear: the human soul hungers for meaning, for wisdom, and Jesus satisfies this hunger. The "sacramental principle" in Christian theology attempts to give language to this idea, by recognizing that through Jesus people encounter God, and that through such celebrations as the Eucharist, we encounter Jesus. But what does this mean? It means, among other things, that through the celebration of the Eucharist, Christians encounter the presence of God on many levels. To put it simply, the Eucharist is a particularly powerful event of prayer for those who allow it to be.

Like the other sacraments, the Eucharist involves both the action of God and the action of people, which means that it, too, can be meaningless to those who do not care about it. Many people have had the experience of participating in the celebration of communion, wondering what the heck they were doing. Teenagers, especially, often have the experience, in the middle of liturgy, when they simply wonder, "Why do my parents make me do this?" Similarly, those who regularly participate in communion sometimes ask themselves, "Why do I keep doing this? What does it mean?" Sacraments are not magic tricks or supernatural shows. They will not dazzle or amaze. So when we are caught up in the repetition of "the same old thing," it is easy to think that even this practice, which Jesus asks us to do in remembrance of him, is boring.

In this respect, the Eucharist is like so many other elements of our lives, the meanings of which often become clearer in retrospect. Consider doing homework in school: How many times do students complain how boring it is? But come graduation day or perhaps finding a new job that requires the skills learned through homework, all that past work becomes meaningful and worthwhile. Or consider those people who practice something day after day, like a sport or a musical instrument, who are sometimes bored by their practice. But when the day comes to perform, the practice itself is recognized as having been important. Most importantly, the relationships we form with people we love grow by the most boring and mundane actions, and yet, when people confront death, they realize how precious those boring, mundane actions are.

Christian spirituality confronts the scope of eternity and the infinite love of God. Sometimes the sacraments do become boring, and this is to be expected to some extent. But as Christians anticipate whatever is subsequent to our short lives, we begin to recognize that even these boring celebrations contribute to our ultimate relationship with God. Over time, it is possible to reflect on how the celebration of the Eucharist in many ways encapsulates the Christian life. It is a challenge to perceive, in the mundane action of sharing food, the love of God poured out through Christ, who nourishes our souls and satiates our hunger. It is a challenge to recognize, in these ordinary people around us, the image of God, which gives to all human beings an exalted dignity that makes them inestimable treasures in the eye of God. It is a challenge to remember that, through the Eucharist, we are transformed by God's grace into perfect human beings, capable of bringing the world about which Jesus preached, simply by following the example of his love. It is indeed a challenge to consider that this same old activity is the very food at the banquet of wisdom, of which we are invited to partake.

The celebration of the Eucharist is ultimately a celebration of God's presence. Food becomes the physical stuff of which our bodies are made, being transformed by energy. Analogously, the human soul is transformed by God, becoming more and more like God. The Eucharist is a celebration of the fact that God seeks intimacy with our souls, our deepest selves—the selves that will develop as a consequence of this intimacy. The experience of being loved by another person can be transformative, allowing us to see ourselves in a new way. The experience of being loved by God is the same: it enables us to understand our true value as human beings, thereby freeing us to become people who, as a result, are able to love others. This is the liberation of the human soul: being released from selfish cravings that can never really be satiated, and being satisfied at the banquet that is God's love. This liberation, moreover, makes us able to reach out to those who are still hungering for that which is more fulfilling, more permanent, more real.

Sex and Marriage

Christian reflection on sex makes sense in light of this theme of liberation. If we begin to truly see ourselves and others as persons of inestimable value to God, then we can never treat anyone except as royalty. Unlike the message of our culture, which says we can use sex for pleasure and then move on, this vision of sex takes on the character of wisdom, i.e., seeing it in relation to eternity. To truly value a person means treating him or her as not merely a body, but as a complex, mysterious human being who desires meaning in life as much as anyone else. The paradox, though, is that this vision does not make sex off-limits; rather, it transforms sex into the human action that has the greatest potential for sacramentality, the greatest potential for manifesting the love of God for another person. Simply put, hands down, people who seek God have the best, most satisfying, most incredible sex.

Whoa! you say. That's a heck of a claim. But studies do support it.[6] And it makes sense: people who love each other deeply, and who make real to each other the very "touch" of God, can tune into the mystery of what it all means. Let's be clear: it is possible (and unfortunately not uncommon) for sex to be no more than a biological function. Some people seem to treat it like an urge that has to be satisfied, like blowing your nose. But where's the fun in that? Even between people who are in love for a time, sex can be great, but only until the relationship fizzles. (Studies indicate that the "romance" period can last, at most, three years. This corresponds to divorce rates in our country.) Some people have had what they thought was great sex, only to look back and feel disappointment, frustration, anger, and even great emotional pain remembering it.

Psychologists emphasize that the power of imagination is the greatest sexual faculty. In other words, a person must be doing more than just acting out something physical. Sex can become boring, routine, ho hum if it is merely a response to a hormonal urge. It has to be fueled by an imagination on fire—in short, it has to have depth if it is to last. Philosopher Paul Ricoeur put it well: "The removal of sexual prohibitions has produced a curious effect . . . sexual experience having become familiar, available, and reduced to a simple biological function becomes rather insignificant."[7] Since sex is so available in this culture, it is quite simply no big deal (or so we think). People hook up sometimes without even knowing each other or expecting to see each other again. Others have sex with people they think they love, then find out in time that the relationship had no depth and thus no sustaining power. In such a context, relationships necessarily suffer, and people get hurt.

One way people respond to this problem of sex becoming routine is to seek new thrills in their sexual experimentation. Another lover, a new way of "doing it," a different place, a few new techniques—there are so many books out there on how to spice up your love life, it's ridiculous. At some point we have to ask whether needing so much spice means that somehow the recipe has been fouled up.

The reason sex founded on a life of prayer is so great is that it becomes an expression of the deepest desires of the human being to encounter mystery in the experience of intimacy with another person. To see in the other the very image of God is to appreciate his or her infinite depth, and to wonder at the other's seeing you in the same way. When sex expresses this vision, it is truly erotic. The word *eros* in Greek means "desire" or "yearning," but in a more general sense of longing for the good, the true, and the beautiful. To say that sex which expresses a spirituality is erotic is to say that it is the physical manifestation of the intense longing of the human heart for the other—not merely the embrace of the other, but the very mystery of the other. When people of prayer have sex, they are expressing real love: something they can't ultimately control, but something that enables them to enter again and again into mystery.

I find it difficult to imagine how this can take place outside of a relationship in which each person promises to love the other forever. Without this promise, the relationship is contingent, and so sex is limited by this contingency: "I love you now, but I'm not sure about tomorrow." But in this age when so many marriages end in divorce, it is difficult to reconcile this seeming ideal picture of marriage with what many people recognize as its reality. How can marriage be sacramental when so often it leads to discord?

We must first recognize that we use the word *marriage,* like the word *love,* to mean many things. So we must be specific. By calling marriage a sacrament, Christians attempt to clarify that it is more than a simple exchange of vows. In this country, there is a minimum understanding that marriage has to involve some kind of legal promise, witnessed by someone who has the proper authority. However, there is nothing further required by many states: the sharing of life, the raising of children, growing old together—all these things are common, but not required. So it is entirely possible for a couple to be married legally for two days, then separate and file for divorce. Is this marriage? The law says yes.

Christians believe that since love demands the intimate sharing of people's lives, it must be taken seriously—and this makes sense. I will not be willing to confide in you, to trust you with my well-being, if I think your friendship is only temporary. I won't want to share with you my deepest secrets, my hopes, the things I'm ashamed of, the things I want to do when I'm old. In short, I won't share my life with you if I believe your friendship is contingent. I must have some assurance that you will be with me no matter what, that your friendship is absolute, that you won't change your mind. Your expression of "unconditional love" for me means that I have nothing to hide from you—I can be totally honest with you about everything, because I know that you will still love me. And because of your friendship, I will have the freedom of being totally honest with myself. I won't have to construct an elaborate façade to hide behind, a mask to wear for you, a persona that obscures my real self. Since you will love me for who I am, I won't feel the need to be someone I'm not. I will be less concerned with being like everyone else, and more concerned with being myself. Because of your love, I will have the freedom of being me, and not some image I present on the outside.

God's love is like this. Since we are made in God's image, we have the capacity to love this same way if we so choose. Christians believe that a real marriage exists when two people love each other in this manner. In short, marriage is the promise that is constantly fulfilled between a man and a woman, that each loves the other the way God loves, for the rest of their lives. This is why it is celebrated by the Church as a sacrament—because it is perhaps the most obvious example of God's presence in people's lives. What better proof of God's love is there than the couple that truly loves each other after fifty, sixty, seventy years of this kind of marriage? It is truly awesome to love another person this way day after day, observing the other growing daily into his or her truest self. It is a paradox that one can grow into the greatest freedom through the act of binding oneself to another.

The difficulty that all people face in the commitment of marriage is that no one can read the future. Certainly, most people who do marry intend for it to be lifelong, but experience tells us that many times people are mistaken. I may intend to love you forever, but how can I know I'll feel the same in ten years? How can I know you will feel the same in ten years?

The mistake is in the equating of "love" and "feeling." The modern understanding is that love is a feeling, and that since feelings change, so does love. But the Christian understanding, with which many have wrestled over the centuries, is that love is a way of being-in-relationship, manifested by actions, which then produces feelings. "Being in love" is not the same as "loving." "Being in love" is a state of romance, of attraction, of desire. Very often, it is sexual. "Love" often is portrayed in movies or books as something that just happens between people—call it chemistry—such that they have a longing just to be with the other person. They sleep together, decide that they have begun a relationship, and go on from there. Somewhere down the road, they get married, and sometimes it works and sometimes it doesn't. The whole picture comes across as being capricious, as though each person is at the mercy of this mysterious "feeling" which might change at any moment, thus ending (or at least jeopardizing) the relationship.

In contrast, the unconditional love that is celebrated in the biblical text, in the sacramental actions of Christians, and between lovers is something that is founded on the concrete decision of a person to be *for* another. "Being in love" is a wonderful experience—it draws people together, it brings to mind one's intense desire to be with another person—but it is merely an appetizer, and it certainly can't nourish an entire relationship for decades. It helps lovers to be conscious of their need for love, and their longing to enter into real love with the other. Ultimately, however, a relationship must be founded on a decision, a choice, if it is going to last: "I will be for you." It is this decision to which a person can return when times are tough. Unlike feelings that can change, a choice to love is something that can constantly be reaffirmed. Moreover, the constant reaffirmation of the decision to love another actually produces those feelings of "being in love." Romance is the celebrated outcome, rather than the cause, of the relationship.

It is no surprise, then, that Christians traditionally have held that sex is best reserved for marriage. This belief is predicated on the sober understanding that sex can be an awesome celebration of unconditional love, but that it makes for a poor foundation for a lasting relationship. Moreover, this view recognizes that since sex can be such a powerful form of intimacy, it has the capacity to distract people from what has to be most important—the communication of unconditional love.

Without love, a sexual relationship will not only be dull, it will fizzle. A relationship that is only about sex can't last. On the other hand, according to the studies mentioned earlier, couples who have strong marriages, especially those based in shared faith, enjoy the best sex.

The focus in Christian marriage, as in all the sacraments, is the unconditional love manifested in the love of people. This kind of love means seeing the human person as one who is infinitely capable of being loved by God, and as one who is infinitely capable of loving others by means of this same love of God. The sometimes pessimistic attitude toward sex outside of marriage is due in part to the knowledge that sex that comes out of a loving relationship is such an important celebration of love, whereas without that kind of a relationship, sex can be trivial and even abusive. Unfortunately, Christians too often have focused on the negative aspects of sexuality rather than emphasizing it positively as a mystery to be celebrated by people who really choose to love one another.

Does this all mean, then, that those who have sex outside of marriage don't love each other? Not necessarily. Today there are many who have active sex lives before marriage, understanding that when the time is right they will get married. The marriage vow is not a magic trick—it doesn't instantly create something that was not present in the relationship before, and it does not suddenly infuse divine love into an already present love shared between two people. It does do two very important things, however, which, together, have an effect on the couple who marry.

First, it asks for a specific promise: "I will love you forever." This promise is one that many couples share in their intimacy before marriage, but in a public setting it takes on a certain formality that makes it more an object of rational decision than a product of high emotion, such as may happen when lovers are enjoying "being in love." This promise is something to which each spouse can return again and again, particularly when times are difficult—and this fact is inevitable. This promise establishes a bedrock upon which the marriage will develop. Since I hold myself to my promise, I must make life choices with my spouse that help us to live up to our promises. In a sense, by making this promise, I am asking others to hold me to being my best self, the self that does what is good even when it is difficult.

Second, the marriage vow makes the relationship public. On a very basic level, it is the public statement, "Sorry, single people; we're both taken." It acknowledges that each is for the other exclusively, and that no other may intrude into the relationship. It is also an affirmation of how marriage is a community endeavor. Couples need each other, but they also need friends, family, and other people in their lives to sustain their commitment to each other. When times are difficult, there can be a tremendous amount of strain on a marriage. It is reassuring to be part of a community that helps a couple in their married life. As noted earlier, the sacraments of the Church are community events. Marriage is certainly something private, but it is also something public, because every couple will need the support of others at some time in their lives. Marriage is a manifestation of grace from one spouse to the other, but it is also a manifestation of grace in the relationships between the couple and the community.

A recent example in our lives will show what I mean. My wife and I adopted our first daughter from China, and after a long journey we returned home to a new life situation with all kinds of new challenges. People came out of the woodwork to help, it seemed—some sent gifts, others made meals for us, others offered babysitting time so we could relax. It was wonderful! What was interesting, I found, was that our "private lives" suddenly seemed very public—but it certainly didn't bother me. On the contrary, it was great to be the object of so much love and care. Here was a way in which our marriage became a manifestation of grace. Everyone involved was "loving," sustaining our marriage by enabling us to be at greater peace together.

The sacramental principle recognizes that real love is contagious. Far from being selfish, it reaches out beyond ourselves and touches others' lives, sometimes in ways that we will never know. In the example, the love between my wife and me moved beyond the confines of our home, even though we never specifically intended for that to happen. In responding to our needs, other people were drawn into what makes this whole situation "sacramental"—people loving people, thereby showing the love of God. It is completely natural. In fact, all the people that pitched in could have been atheists, and it wouldn't have mattered one bit. What is important is that through the eyes of faith, we saw the goodness of God in the good actions of others.

Because Christians recognize the superabundance of real love, there is some concern over things that look like love but are not. Again, this is why I suspect there is a good deal of pessimism regarding sex. Very often it looks like love but is not. People can be fooled by sex, thinking it is love, and so it becomes hurtful. And often it is the more vulnerable person who is hurt, the one who thought love was there but later discovers that it was only temporary. To be sure, sex sometimes is only an object in itself: people don't want to love, which takes work; they're interested in only the sex. Why is this wrong? Because people don't "have sex"; rather, they "have" another person in a sexual relationship, and it is wrong to use people. In our culture, we have mistakenly made sex into an object, as though it were something distinct from the person with whom we share it. But it is no more possible to separate sex from the person than it is to separate conversation from the person. To engage in sex is to engage in a relationship—and some relationships are more destructive than others. All our relationships contribute to the kind of person we become, and so it is important to value our relationships.

Christian spirituality is fundamentally based on the theme of relationships: between God, others, and self. It is modeled on an understanding of a God who is relational—Father, Son, and Holy Spirit—who draws us into relationship, so that by means of relationship we may come to share in the life of God. Love, in this context, is the very substance of relationship, the stuff that enables us to know God. Thus, it is no surprise that Christians take seriously the practice of loving, and are wary of things that look like love but are not. It may be said that Christian spirituality is ultimately "love training," similar to the training undertaken by athletes or musicians who are preparing for and perfecting gifts and skills. At their best, ministers and leaders are "love coaches," and the Bible is a kind of "love training manual." But before this analogy limps along too far, let me explain further in a more concrete fashion.

Understanding that the human being is created to the image and likeness of God, Christians seek to model their lives after the life of God, which is most clearly revealed by Jesus Christ. Since the stories about Jesus' life focus on his loving people by teaching them, healing them, dying for them, and rising for them, we too seek to make our lives examples of this kind of self-giving. There is a sermon by St. Augustine that draws an analogy between the practice of the spirituality of self-giving and the title of this chapter, "Breaking Bread Together." Augustine says, referring to the eucharistic bread, that we are the grains of wheat crushed by the divine bread maker, transforming us into the bread that will be shared by all people. By allowing ourselves to be so transformed by God, we become an offering to those who are spiritually hungry and who need to be fed by love. By persevering in faith, hope, and love, we come to know ourselves in relation to others and to God, and we become the bread for the world.

For Group Discussion

1. Do you consider spirituality to be a community activity? How is your own spirituality affected by community?
2. What are your experiences of liturgy? Does liturgy contribute to your spirituality? If so, how? If not, why?
3. Have you chosen to be part of a church community? How have you come to your decision?
4. If you are part of a church, what are the distinguishing features of your community? How is it unique from other communities of faith?
5. How does your faith challenge you to be countercultural? In what ways does your spirituality lead you to make choices different from people around you?
6. What are your reflections on the way the word *sacrament* is used in this chapter? How can you identify with the idea in your own experience?
7. Identify an experience of conversion in your own life, either sudden or gradual. How is your spirituality different today compared to what it was five or ten years ago?
8. Who is an example of a person whose work is sacramental? Do you think it is possible to manifest God's love to people even without specifically intending to?
9. What is your reaction to the claim that people of faith enjoy the best sex? Do you see a connection between spirituality and sex?

CHAPTER FIVE

Feasting at the Banquet: Living in Faith, Hope, and Love

"Come to the...banquet."
—MATTHEW 22:4

The guests are met, the feast is set:
Mays't hear the merry din.
—S. T. COLERIDGE

A theme repeated throughout the Bible is that being with God is like a party! Sometimes Christians portray a God who comes across as a cosmic killjoy, not letting us have any fun. "Don't do this"; "Thou shalt not that." There was a character on the program *Saturday Night Live* some years ago called the "church lady," who was this kind of person: she attributed to the devil any evidence of a person having a good time. "Who's telling you to have a good time? Could it be *Satan?*"

I'm happy to report that Jesus was not such a prude. On the contrary, he was once accused of getting a little out of hand with his eating and drinking (see Matthew 11:19). In fact, we often see him dining and relaxing with people, having a good time. In John's Gospel, Jesus' first miracle is the act of changing water into wine, so that the people at a wedding banquet could keep having fun. Clearly Jesus was the kind of person who could have a good time. His invitation for people to respond to God used the theme of a divine banquet, an eternal party that God wants to share with those who love him.

Jesus used the terms "the kingdom of God" or "the reign of God" to refer to this invitation. In the Gospel of Mark, for example, Jesus' first public words are: "The time is fulfilled, and the kingdom of God has come near; repent, and believe in the good news" (1:15). As noted earlier, Jesus' words leave us with a tension, though: this kingdom is *already* here among people, but it's also something that *will* happen sometime in the future; it is not yet accomplished. Christians must wrestle with the theme of the "already but not yet" in their attempt to make meaning out of their own lives. How can an authentic Christian spirituality transform our lives now, and what hope does it offer in the future?

This chapter explores the kingdom of God as a banquet to which God invites all people. This biblical image offers us an opportunity to reflect on the tension of the "already but not yet" and how this tension can impact the lives of people who still wrestle with the question of how to live as one who seeks to know God through Jesus.

Faith

> One of the dinner guests . . . said to him, "Blessed is anyone who will eat bread in the kingdom of God!" Then Jesus said to him, "Someone gave a great dinner and invited many. At the time for the dinner he sent his slave to say to those who had been invited, 'Come; for everything is ready now.' But they all alike began to make excuses. The first said to him, 'I have bought a piece of land, and I must go out and see it; please accept my regrets.' Another said, 'I have bought five yoke of oxen, and I am going to try them out; please accept my regrets.' Another said, 'I have just been married, and therefore I cannot come.' So the slave returned and reported this to his master. Then the owner of the house became angry and said to his slave, 'Go out at once into the streets and lanes of the town and bring in the

poor, the crippled, the blind, and the lame.' And
the slave said, 'Sir, what you ordered has been
done, and there is still room.' Then the master said
to the slave, 'Go out into the roads and lanes, and
compel people to come in, so that my house may
be filled. For I tell you, none of those who were
invited will taste my dinner.'" (Luke 14:15–24)

Faith is the response to the invitation of God to participate in the
banquet. Through faith, we recognize that God loves us first, and that
in order to know God we need only heed the invitation. The parable is
a kind of story about salvation history—and many have refused to
acknowledge the invitation. But those who are considered "least"
among people are the ones who do respond; those are the ones who fill
the banquet hall.

We use the generic term *faith* in a similarly confusing way to our
use of the word *love*. We speak of faith in our favorite team, in the stock
market, in our friends. And, indeed, there is a common theme in these
different understandings of what faith entails: the recognition that I am
powerless over something important to me. There are many times in
our lives when we want to have certainty about something: Is this the
right choice? Should I trust this person? What will the test be like? In
these situations, though, we are frustrated precisely because we know
that we cannot know the answer. So what do we do? We choose either
to retain or sacrifice our power.

When I choose to trust someone, I hand over power to that person,
expecting something in return. I trust a bank with my money; I trust
my doctor with my health; I trust an airline pilot to deliver me safely
to my destination. Faith, however, is deeper than trust, for it means
handing over power without expectation, and this can be scary.

Every time I go into have my car repaired, for example, there's a
part of me that is frustrated: How do I know they're telling me the
truth? They could be making up something so they can get more
money out of me. If I had the time and inclination, of course, I could
take the car to different places and see if they all agree. Or I could learn
exactly how my car works and fix it myself. At least then I might have
some greater degree of certainty about what to do. Instead, because I

can't spend a great deal time on my car, I decide to trust , simply because I can't spend more energy on it. I hand over power to the mechanics, but with the expectation that I will get something in return.

Faith is a deeper kind of trust. I recently asked a friend to travel several hours during a weekend to be with us during an important time. When I called to make the request, I knew that I was asking a lot of this person, who had a very busy life. But it was important to us that she be there, so I put myself in a vulnerable position, basically saying, "We need you," thereby making rejection possible. But this friend responded, "I'll be there," and her presence made a big difference. In this situation, I acted on faith: I chose to hand over my power to bring about a desired consequence. The result was not expectation of something in return, as with trust, but rather hope that my friend would honor and respond to our need.

A final example of the way people trust is the relationship that can develop between a parent and a child. Imagine a child who is learning to swim. The father shows his daughter what swimming looks like, then holds her as she learns to kick and move her arms. At a certain point, however, the man tells his daughter that it is time for her to try it by herself. He lets go, and she panics and starts sinking. She is frightened, of course, but her father catches her before she hurts herself. He speaks to her with reassurance and encouragement: "Don't worry. Try again. I'll help you if you need me. You can do it." She doesn't want to, but she eventually tries again, succeeds, and makes her father proud. The young girl has faith that her father asks of her only that which is good for her, even though she might not be ready right then.

The biblical metaphor of God as a father highlights some of these same dynamics. God wishes our good, and supports our failures. God encourages us and loves us dearly. Most important is the fact that God is a father who offers us opportunities to trust, opportunities to respond in faith to his love manifested sacramentally through the love of people in our lives. When spouses love each other, when friends love each other, when siblings love each other, when complete strangers love each other: all of these are sacramental opportunities to respond to the love of God by acting on faith rather than being skeptical. When someone says something nice to me, I can choose to think that the person has ulterior motives and wants something from me, or I can choose to respond in kind by trusting that the person is simply being a good person. In choosing the latter, I act faithfully.

As noted in the first chapter, there is a kind of "faithful knowing" that transforms the way we view the world. Instead of the world being a place where we are always in competition, trying to get ahead of everyone else who is trying to get ahead of us, we begin to see the world as filled with grace. To be sure, adopting the first worldview is easy: we must assert our own interests or be trampled. But the second worldview enables us to understand the different motivations people have, and to recognize loving action as a gift when it happens.

On the deepest level, we speak of "faith in God" as a disposition through which our entire life becomes a continuous attempt to respond to God's love. We have faith that God ultimately wants our good like a loving father wants the good of his child. We understand that this faith does not mean that we can expect everything to go our way: sometimes we have to thrash around a little before we learn to swim. We certainly do not believe that we will never suffer—even Jesus was not exempt from pain. But we do believe that despite suffering, there is resurrection. Faith is the gift that enables us to persevere in hope because through faith, we believe that the ending to our stories is good, even if the middle chapters are difficult. It encompasses the dynamic dialogue between the faithful person and God, the constant exchange by which our hunger for meaning is satiated by God's wisdom. In time, faith becomes the very habit of our life, even if at first it seems more like a leap into mystery.

Christian faith holds that God always welcomes those who respond to his invitation, and that moreover, he rejoices at those who come back to him.

> [The lost son] set off and went to his father. But while he was still far off, his father saw him and was filled with compassion; he ran and put his arms around him and kissed him. . . . [t]he father said to his slaves, 'Quickly, bring out a robe—the best one—and put it on him; put a ring on his finger and sandals on his feet. And get the fatted calf and kill it, and let us eat and celebrate; for

> this son of mine was dead and is alive again; he
> was lost and is found!' And they began to cele-
> brate." (Luke 15:20; 22–24)

The act of Christian faith is simply the acknowledgment of God's love for us. The son who returned in the parable of the prodigal son was no saint—in fact, he was still acting selfishly when he decided to return to the father. He was more in touch with his hunger than with the pain he'd caused his family. But the point is, the son returned, and the father, who had been eagerly waiting, saw him and rejoiced, and convinced him that not only was he welcome but his presence was cause for a great feast. God loves us in this same "prodigal" fashion, and is able to transform our reluctance into celebration.

Throughout the Gospel there are examples of Jesus reaching out to people who were not particularly good or holy or religious—ordinary people who often sought to be good but who also made mistakes.

> When the Pharisees saw this, they said to his dis-
> ciples, "Why does your teacher eat with tax col-
> lectors and sinners?" But when he heard this, he
> said, "Those who are well have no need of a
> physician, but those who are sick. Go and learn
> what this means, 'I desire mercy, not sacrifice.'
> For I have come to call not the righteous but sin-
> ners." (Matthew 9:11–13)

People are touched by Jesus because he accepts them where they are, loving them as human beings created by God. People respond in faith to him simply because they choose to accept that Jesus' words are true, and that he genuinely loves them and is not merely putting on an act. In different places we find Jesus commenting on the faith of people—and almost every time, his comment is directed to a person who, by the standards of the day, is not considered a particularly good person.

> When he entered Capernaum, a centurion came
> to him, appealing to him and saying, "Lord, my

servant is lying at home paralyzed, in terrible distress." And he said to him, "I will come and cure him." The centurion answered, "Lord, I am not worthy to have you come under my roof; but only speak the word, and my servant will be healed. For I also am a man under authority, with soldiers under me; and I say to one, 'Go,' and he goes, and to another, 'Come,' and he comes, and to my slave, 'Do this,' and the slave does it." When Jesus heard him, he was amazed and said to those who followed him, "Truly I tell you, in no one in Israel have I found such faith." (Matthew 8:5–10)

. . .

Now there was a woman who had been suffering from hemorrhages for twelve years. She had endured much under many physicians, and had spent all that she had; and she was no better, but rather grew worse. She had heard about Jesus, and came up behind him in the crowd and touched his cloak, for she said, "If I but touch his clothes, I will be made well." Immediately her hemorrhage stopped; and she felt in her body that she was healed of her disease. Immediately aware that power had gone forth from him, Jesus turned about in the crowd and said, "Who touched my clothes?" And his disciples said to him, "You see the crowd pressing in on you; how can you say, 'Who touched me?' He looked all around to see who had done it. But the woman, knowing what had happened to her, came in fear and trembling, fell down before him, and told him the whole truth. He said to her, "Daughter, your faith has made you well; go in peace, and be healed of your disease." (Mark 5:25–34)

In the first story, the centurion is a Roman, meaning he is a foreigner and a member of the military establishment that terrorizes the Jews. He is of a different religious background and is held in contempt by many of Jesus' contemporaries. Yet Jesus recognizes his act of love for his servant, and also recognizes that it took faith for him to come to Jesus in the first place. Imagine the scene: having little experience with Jewish religion of the time, it is likely that the centurion simply hears that Jesus is a healer. Perhaps he has no particular interest in religion at all. But he does care about his servant, and so goes to seek out Jesus. It is likely that he has to spend some considerable energy just finding this itinerant preacher, and moreover he has to travel among the locals to get close to him. As a military officer, he is unaccustomed to the ways of the people, and probably has to struggle with the difference in language: his being Latin, Jesus' being Aramaic. Yet he accomplishes what he sets out to do: he asks Jesus to heal his servant, believing that Jesus can do it even without seeing the man. The centurion has no proof that this will happen, but only the stories that other people have told him about this person. Surprisingly, his words to Jesus are humble, uncharacteristic of a person in his place: "I am not worthy." In seeking out Jesus, the centurion recognizes, on some level, that he has not been a perfect person. But instead of keeping to himself, he admits this and asks for Jesus' help anyway.

The faith to which Jesus makes reference in his response to the centurion is difficult to identify. Is it the centurion's love for his servant? Is it his trust in Jesus' power? Is it his self-effacement? Is it his courage? Is it some combination of all these? The story raises questions about faith even as it gives us a good example of it.

The second story, from the Gospel of Mark, is similar. The woman with a hemorrhage is also courageous, persistent, and humble. An interesting point about this story is that she doesn't particularly want to talk to Jesus—she just wants to be cured of her affliction. She is positively afraid of this public person who seems so daunting and holy. Hers is almost a superstition: "If I just touch his clothing, I'll be cured." Is she being selfish? Is she trying to take advantage of Jesus? Her reaction when Jesus looks for her is "fear and trembling." In the first century Jewish world, it is common to believe that illness and disability are punishments from God, visited upon people who themselves or whose parents are sinners. This woman, then, probably sees herself as a person cursed by God. Yet something convinces her that this man Jesus is the one who can release her from this curse by curing her. Call it just plain hopefulness, even without proof, again based on what others have told her about him, and perhaps from something she sees him do. She chooses to try touching him to see what happens. The result is twofold: she is cured, and Jesus tells her to go and live her life in peace.

In both stories, the people start with an attitude of hopefulness: maybe this Jesus will give me what I seek. They seek him out, literally traveling to meet him so that they might find out what he can do. In other words, each person already has a kind of "faith" in Jesus, based on their hope that he is of God. What Jesus does for them is a response to their already present faith. He does not give them faith; instead, he recognizes that faith is already at work in them, and that it is through this faith that they find what they have sought from him.

These people are much like people today. These are not stories about extraordinary people, like world leaders, tycoons, movie stars, or intellectuals. Rather, they are ordinary people, like all of us, who want a good life. The centurion is a good man who cares for someone close to him. The woman is someone who just wants to be rid of her sickness. Both experience spiritual hungers that we all understand. It is common to yearn for friendship, good health, security, fun, a direction in life—all these are desires of the human heart reaching ultimately for God, and Jesus understands. He does not ask that these people make any solemn profession of religious belief before he answers them, nor does he make sure they believe the same things he does. He simply responds to their spiritual needs with love. In effect, his ability to touch these people in their moments of need shows them that God loves them, cares for them, and wants to be loved by them.

The manifestation of faith in both stories comes as the result of each person recognizing his or her need and dependence on God. Jesus is able to love these people precisely because they make themselves vulnerable. The same is true for us; unless we acknowledge our spiritual needs, we will never seek healing from God. We are so accustomed to covering our needs, pretending they don't exist, distracting ourselves from them, that we never give God the chance to touch us in the way he touches the centurion and the woman with a hemorrhage. We must admit that we are lonely, hurt, betrayed, weak, afraid, and helpless if we are ever going to seek God's healing. And doing this is enormously difficult, especially if we have been disappointed in our lives before. To summon the courage as did the characters in the biblical stories is also to set ourselves up for discouragement: to allow God to heal us is also to give God the chance to fail. But we are promised again and again that God will not fail, that he will never fail if we invite him into our lives. Rather, God "through grace gave us eternal comfort and good hope" (2 Thessalonians 2:16) because he has chosen us to be his own, even before we were born.

The real difficulty in acknowledging our spiritual brokenness is that it seems so counterintuitive to dwell on the negative things in life. We are so accustomed to emphasizing the positive, wanting to get over whatever is bothering us so we can move on with our lives. Many, in fact, treat problems by not dealing with them at all, pretending they don't exist, and distracting themselves with more and more activities. After all, ours is a busy culture—we love to work (even though we always grumble against it) and have a real problem just sitting down and being quiet. So we fail to notice our spiritual hungers and, instead, focus on "self-improvement," as if learning a new language, a new kind of workout, or a new diet will solve the problems with our souls. Self-improvement, to be sure, is not a bad thing; but it can help us forget that we are hurting deep within, and have never sought the healing of these soul wounds. As a result, people construct elaborate personae that are more and more separated from their real selves, the people with whom they contend when they sit alone, undistracted by others. In silence, we must confront our real selves, and in this silence we sometimes find that our real selves have been suffering from neglect.

A difference between the stories of the centurion and the woman with the hemorrhage is that each person had a different interest. The centurion's faith saved his servant; the woman's faith saved herself. In this context, what was "saved" was physical health; "salvation" here means the ability to lead a good, healthy life. But elsewhere, "salvation" is used in a more profound sense as it relates to faith.

> For I am not ashamed of the gospel; it is the
> power of God for salvation to everyone who has

faith . . . For in it the righteousness of God is
revealed through faith for faith; as it is written,
"The one who is righteous will live by faith."
(Romans 1:16–17)

Saint Paul's reference here to "salvation" is not to physical healing,
and his reference to faith leading to life is different from what we find
in the stories of the centurion and the woman. Paul's idea addresses the
spiritual pain that people confront, recognizing that this pain is no less
real than physical pain. Throughout our lives there are times when we
cannot make sense of the wrongs we undergo. These wrongs leave us
wounded, incapable of returning to the state of being we enjoyed
before the wound. Sometimes we bring these wounds upon ourselves,
injuring our own souls by treating them as unimportant: this we call
sin. At other times, we are injured by life circumstances: death, sickness, loss. And then there are those times when we are hurt by others.
All of these cause us suffering and make us wonder how to understand
it all. When Paul speaks of "salvation," then, he proclaims that the
gospel, the good news about Jesus, saves our souls. This good news
enables us to know that Jesus is able to save our souls from the suffering we endure, and gives people the hope that they, too, might seek
Jesus and, like the woman, encounter his healing. But it also gives people hope that they might act like the centurion, finding Jesus so that he
might heal someone else who won't (or can't) seek him alone.

But what does this mean? It is one thing to say "Jesus saves" and
another to experience Jesus saving reality in our lives. Saving us from
what? For what? Why do we need to be saved, and why is faith what
brings this about?

We are saved from meaninglessness. We are saved from suffering
that does nothing but make us suffer more. We are saved from dying a
death that is permanent. We are saved from hurting other people; from
continuing to hurt ourselves; from going on with a life that is drudg-
ery; from becoming creatures who cannot love others. We are saved
from misery.

We are saved for life. We are saved for intimacy with God; for the
sake of our ultimate happiness. We are saved because God created us

and doesn't want us to go to waste. We are saved so that others might be saved, so that our lives can become beautiful.

God is the artist who made us works of art, beautiful and majestic. Suffering is like spray paint, covering us with a kind of film that, in some cases, leaves us unrecognizable. But rather than throwing us away and starting over, God wants to save us, so he removes from us everything that has tarnished us. Why? Because a work of art is irreplaceable and invaluable to the artist.

Faith is what *allows* God to save us, because God does not do anything against our will. Faith, then, is our willingness to let God save us. With time, faith becomes the conviction that God will save us, that the love of God *does* save us. Eventually, faith becomes that burning desire to give back our life to God out of sheer joy for saving us.

Hope

Hope allows us to look forward to our being saved from suffering. The centurion hoped; the woman with a hemorrhage hoped. Hope arises not only from the recognition of one's spiritual hunger but also from the heart's desire that this hunger be satiated. Hope is also a gift of God, one in which all people share when they think positively toward the future. The seed of hope exists in all people, but blooms in faith in those who respond to the love of God manifested in Jesus.

Hope is what motivates people in all walks of life to make themselves better. Hope gives rise to dieting fads, keeps workout facilities and travel agents in business, feeds the market for self-help books, and makes students want to get an education. Hope is what pushes us to look for that one person with whom we want to spend our lives, even if the process of searching becomes tiresome or painful. Hope is what sustains the artist who can barely feed herself, the father who works sixteen hours so his kids can go to a safe school, the mother who waits day after day in bed just so she can give birth to a healthy baby. Hope offers us something to hold on to after tragedies, failures, and disappointments that buffet us throughout our lives. Hope lies underneath anything good and beautiful in the human experience, and is the missing element in the dark side of life.

Human beings are naturally hopeful. We want something to hope for, because hope enables us to form a vision of our lives that gives rise to meaning. Adults who want to understand what children hope for often ask "What do you want to be when you grow up?" Teachers and academic counselors often ask students what they will do when they finish school, thus encouraging students to think about what they hope for in life. In these examples, hope is a kind of compass pointing toward a possible future. Hope represents a direction, even if one cannot have certainty about it—and in this way, hope is similar to faith. As much as we would like to have control over the future, though, it is impossible. We cannot know what will happen; the best we can do is make life choices that we discern will move us in the direction of our hopes.

The loss of hope is the greatest tragedy in human experience, for without hope there is the loss of meaning and joy. When people lose hope, they lose a sense of direction in life, and so turn to the present moment with the attitude that the only good is to be derived from immediate pleasure and avoidance of pain. Unfortunately, our instant-gratification culture feeds this immediate desire. Pleasure itself is not bad, to be sure, but if it is the only reality driving life, then we likely will not seek the source of real hope. Moreover, pleasures themselves tend to be fleeting and often hinder us from seeking the things that genuinely nourish our souls. Pleasure is like junk food: it can be good, but we need something more substantial.

Many people in our culture have lost hope. They are unable to love others, because love demands work, which is sometimes unpleasant. They are similarly unable to love themselves, because they do not see themselves as having any lasting meaning or value beyond the moment. Their lives are led not in constant vigilance for that which is good and life-giving, but in a kind of reactionary mode, meaning they wish to have experiences and derive as much pleasure as possible. It is not surprising, then, that many people turn to the novel experiences provided by drugs or the pursuit of sex, while others seek to try every new thing that comes along, be it skydiving or exotic travel or the "perfect" job. Because human beings are hopeful, we naturally reach out for those things we believe will give us hope—but we often are mistaken. We fix on something that delights us for a time, but eventually we realize that it doesn't meet our deepest needs—and we move on to something else.

Over time, this process of hoping and losing hope leads to disillusionment, which is so characteristic of life in our postmodern culture. What we need, then, is a source of hope that transcends the vagaries of our hurried lives, that offers us lasting hope not only in the present moment but over the course of our entire lives.

Jesus used two similes to address this deep desire of people:

> "The kingdom of heaven is like treasure hidden in a field, which someone found and hid; then in his joy he goes and sells all that he has and buys that field.
>
> "Again, the kingdom of heaven is like a merchant in search of fine pearls; on finding one pearl of great value, he went and sold all that he had and bought it." (Matthew 13:44–46)

Jesus teaches that faith gives people such powerful hope that they need nothing else to be happy. Both of the images he uses are economic, suggesting that the best way to understand this kind of hope is to relate it to our common hopes for financial security now and in the future. Another way of thinking about it might be to use the modern example of the stock market. Imagine you were living in the early 1900s and had the ability to predict the future. If you were offered the chance to buy stock in a company that sold a new drink called Coca-Cola, you would sell everything you owned, probably borrow more, and sink every penny into the stock. Eventually, you would be rich beyond your dreams. So it is with faith, Jesus tells us. If we could read the future and understand what God has in store for us, we would devote every last element of our lives to our faith in him. This is the kind of hope that gives life to Christian spirituality.

Where does this hope come from? As articulated in the Scriptures and testified to by people throughout history, it comes from God's promise. Hope was established in the covenant with Abraham, manifested in the kingdom of David, emphasized by the prophets, and lived by Jesus. The psalmist wrote the following prayer as a testimonial to hope in God:

> In you, O LORD, I take refuge;
> > let me never be put to shame.
> In your righteousness deliver me and rescue me;
> > incline your ear to me and save me.
> Be to me a rock of refuge,
> > a strong fortress, to save me,
> > for you are my rock and my fortress.
>
> Rescue me, O my God, from the hand of the wicked,
> > from the grasp of the unjust and cruel.
> For you, O Lord, are my hope,
> > my trust, O LORD, from my youth.
> Upon you I have leaned from my birth;
> > it was you who took me from my mother's womb.
> My praise is continually of you (Psalm 71:1–6).

Notice that in the eighth and ninth lines, the psalmist makes reference to some kind of suffering at the hands of enemies. Often, it is through the experience of suffering that we find we must rely on God, because we have no one else to whom we can turn. Christian hope is the gift that enables us to have assurance of God's love even in these dire circumstances. It does not mean that God can make all suffering go away, but rather that God loves us and is with us through the experience of suffering. For some, this is small consolation. But throughout the Scriptures, we are reminded that people do suffer even when they are loved by God. The stories of Job, Hosea, Paul, and others, for example, remind us that God does not keep his beloved from suffering. But these stories also show us examples of people who remain faithful through the experience of suffering, simply because they cannot do otherwise, for to lose faith would be to lose the very meaning of life.

This hope is made explicit in the New Testament by those who reflect upon the overcoming of death through Jesus' Resurrection.

> Blessed be the God and Father of our Lord Jesus
> Christ! By his great mercy he has given us a new
> birth into a living hope through the resurrection
> of Jesus Christ from the dead . . . (1 Peter 1:3).

There is an easily understood psychology of people who first believed in the resurrection of the dead. If suffering hinders our lives, then surely the greatest suffering is death itself. But if death becomes something not to fear—but rather to embrace as a passage into eternal happiness—then this is cause for great hope.

The early Christians had no fear of death. They ministered to people with contagious diseases, when others simply cast them out of their houses and communities to prevent infection. They sang songs of joy when they faced the lions, as punishment under Roman rule. They praised God when they were horribly martyred, facing death with hope because they trusted in the truth of the Resurrection. For them, suffering was not something to be feared, because it was through suffering that they could fully share in the life promised by Jesus.

At times, this understanding of suffering took on unsavory aspects, leading some to believe that suffering itself was to be sought and that happiness was contrary to the gospel. In retrospect, Christians today understand that these are not good conclusions. Rather, when we encounter suffering, or when we share in the sufferings of others, we can more deeply share in the love of God which will, in the end, save us from all suffering.

For many, the talk of heaven is little more than an idealistic tendency to sugarcoat the reality of evil in the world. To be sure, some use the idea of heaven as a way to escape the world. But the hope for heaven is not to be set in contrast to the reality of life here and now. Instead, the hope for heaven is a kind of final chapter to the stories of our lives. In any story, the ending is what makes it either a comedy or a tragedy, and all the suffering along the way serves to highlight what the final outcome will be. Christian hope does not suggest that this life is of no consequence: the kingdom is "already but not yet." On the contrary, Christian hope insists that this life is of such importance that our eternity depends on it. The promise of the Resurrection enables people to understand that all their sufferings now strengthen their commitment to life: if I can live through this suffering, I love life dearly and wish to preserve it forever. Moreover, the promise of eternal life without suffering allows us to believe that our suffering is not ultimately without meaning, for it is through perseverance that we are moved closer to joy.

Hope encourages us to think of suffering as that which will enable us to experience joy to an even greater degree. In life, the experience of deprivation is hard, but once it is over, it makes us conscious of what is good in what we formerly considered a deficiency. Those who were once hungry really know the joy of good food. Those who were once sick can appreciate the vigor of health. Those who were lonely will truly love those who love them. Suffering itself is horrible, but after suffering there can be great joy. Life itself may be miserable at times, but resurrection will be pure joy.

Like all spiritual gifts, hope is not easily recognizable by those who have no experience of it. Those who have no faith and no hope are not necessarily to blame for it. Those who die without hope, those who take their own lives, those who have never really been loved did not choose their suffering. It is true that we are called to persevere through suffering, but some are never given the chance to hear the call, perhaps because some other person has failed to utter it to them. Trusting in God's promise is possible only if one has understood what that promise means. In hope we pray for those without hope, so that like the centurion's servant .they too might know the healing power of God through the intercession of others.

With God there is hope, and without God there is none. Even those who reject the God preached by religious hypocrites can sometimes cling to hope—in the goodness of people, in the reality of love, in the belief that life has meaning—and in so doing implicitly acknowledge the reality of God. Trusting in the ability of people to do good is itself a manifestation of this implicit hope, for it is an acknowledgment of a moral law, which cannot exist without God. Indeed, the very reality of love testifies to hope in God, for without such hope there could be no love. Unselfish action happens for reasons that sometimes people cannot even name, for as Pascal said, "The heart has its reasons which reason can never know." But people do act unselfishly, not out of instinct and for no personal gain, but simply because there is in them a conscience that yearns for goodness. When a person truly loves another, it arises out of the hope that such action is of some ultimate consequence: it is the "right" thing to do. Our obligations to family, our commitment to promises, our recognition that harming others is wrong: all these are evidence of our basic hope rising into love. This hope, of course, need not be named or even recognized for it to be a motivating factor in our lives. There are good and holy people who do not name God, but manifest God's love no less in their lives because they hope. Perhaps they have even rejected what religious authorities have taught them, but what they reject in their minds they still affirm in their lives of love. Where there is charity and love, God is there—and where there is hope, there is charity and love.

So what good is religion? It gives us the language with which to identify our hopes, and moreover, it gives us the discipline with which to pursue them. Imagine the athlete who yearns to win an Olympic medal. He has fixed his hope on the ideal, standing upon the platform and hearing the national anthem being played on his behalf. This hope gives a structure to his life. He knows that there are certain things he must choose to do: get good coaching, move to a training site, engage in a strict regimen of training, diet, and rest. He also knows that there are certain things that are now prohibited, or at least deferred: he cannot live a carefree life, eat and drink whatever he likes, start a new and time-consuming job, or even expect a normal family life. He makes tremendous sacrifices, which themselves can be enormously painful, but which he chooses in the name of his hope. Religious faith is similar. It enables us to name our hope, and helps us to identify the things that faith impels us to choose, such as the disciplined life of prayer, loving service, and community. It also helps us to recognize the things we must sacrifice in pursuit of our hope: selfish action, our false selves, our idolatrous images of God. Religious faith is about the structured life of a community in pursuit of its hope.

Another example serves to illustrate the relationship between religion and hope. Imagine now an entire team seeking an Olympic medal. There arise many different problems for this team: Who will lead the team? How should the individuals of the team act together as a single unit? What plans should the team follow in pursuit of their hope? That which is difficult for the individual's hope is even more complicated for the community's hope. Notice that these problems parallel those faced by a religious tradition: issues of authority, morality, doctrine. But the key point is that all these problems arise precisely because the team wishes to pursue the shared goal of victory. One can imagine that different teams will address the issues of authority, morality, and doctrine differently—some with greater success than others—but all must face them because they arise out of the very human dynamics of community.

Christians share the hope of eternal life, but this shared hope gives rise to conflicts of authority, morality, and doctrine. Authority questions include: Who should lead us? Priests? elders? bishops? the pope? women? homosexuals? educated people? people with a certain spirituality? Morality questions include: What must we do to follow Jesus? How must we love our neighbor? When is sex moral? When is killing justified? How are we forgiven by God? How should we forgive each other? Doctrine questions include: Was Jesus God or a man adopted by God? How do we recognize the Holy Spirit? How should we celebrate the Last Supper? How must we initiate new Christians? All these questions are important, and the ongoing dialogue among Christians gives vigor to faith and enables people to maintain hope. Unfortunately, many see the disagreements among Christians as evidence that the questions themselves are meaningless. This is a hasty conclusion, nor does it absolve us from authentically seeking answers. Authentic hope demands that we answer these and other difficult questions, because we are impelled toward our hope with a zeal similar to that of the Olympic team. We cannot give up, nor can we simply abandon the team and pursue the hope on our own. It is impossible to love God without also loving one's neighbors! (cf. 1 John 4:20)

Hope, then, must give rise to love, for love is what enables individuals to understand themselves in relationship with other people in pursuit of ultimate hope. If I, as a member of the team, understand that I can achieve my hope of winning a medal only if I and everyone else contribute to win, I will seek to improve myself and others. Instead of seeking to beat everyone else on my team, I will seek to enhance the performance of my entire team. I will, in short, care about the team as a whole. I will learn to love each person individually, and thus the team as a community. I will, at times, sacrifice my own desires for the good of the team, and I will practice with them rather than by myself. I will subordinate my own judgment to that of the coach, and I will expect that the others will do the same. I will do as I am told to the extent that it enables the whole team to succeed.

Religion is necessarily based on the notion of shared hope in a community, and as such it involves a kind of discipline of love. The spiritual life is like life in general: there are ups and downs, and so this discipline can itself remind us of our hopes during times when it is easy to abandon them. The athlete's hope is only as strong as the worst day on which she wants to give up: discipline urges her to work harder in the times when it is most dismal, because the hope offers an unsurpassable reward. The religious person's hope enables her to recognize times of depression and desolation, and press on in faith because her hope is eternal. Sometimes, though, people need others to remind them to maintain faith. In the face of incredible suffering, people can lose faith without the strength and support of others enabling them to cling to a sliver of hope. Religion is a commitment to a way of believing, but more fundamentally it is (or can be) a commitment to a community of people who share not only hope, but also understandings of authority, morality, and doctrine which serve to move them toward that hope.

Love

Saint Paul writes most eloquently of love:

> If I speak in the tongues of mortals and of angels, but do not have love, I am a noisy gong or a clanging cymbal. And if I have prophetic powers, and understand all mysteries and all knowledge, and if I have all faith, so as to remove mountains, but do not have love, I am nothing. If I give away all my possessions, and if I hand over my body so that I may boast, but do not have love, I gain nothing.
>
> Love is patient; love is kind; love is not envious or boastful or arrogant or rude. It does not insist on its own way; it is not irritable or resentful; it does not rejoice in wrongdoing, but rejoices in the truth. It bears all things, believes all things, hopes all things, endures all things.
>
> Love never ends. But as for prophecies, they will come to an end; as for tongues, they will

cease; as for knowledge, it will come to an end. For we know only in part, and we prophesy only in part; but when the complete comes, the partial will come to an end. When I was a child, I spoke like a child, I thought like a child, I reasoned like a child; when I became an adult, I put an end to childish ways. For now we see in a mirror, dimly, but then we will see face to face. Now I know only in part; then I will know fully, even as I have been fully known. And now faith, hope, and love abide, these three; and the greatest of these is love (1 Corinthians 13:1–13).

Love is the central virtue in Christian spirituality because only through love do we come to know God, other people, and ultimately ourselves. Love is the very stuff that enables human beings to exist uniquely in the image of God, to share in the very life of God, to even taste eternity in the present moment. Love is the ultimate mystery, the depth of which can never be plumbed by human understanding, but it is also the most obvious truth that can be known by even the simplest child. Love is the invitation into life itself, and it is the lack of love that throws people into the most abject pits of despair. It is the favored subject of novelists, poets, artists, musicians, sages, and charlatans, because it is that to which human beings are drawn again and again through all epochs of history. Love is eminently human, supremely human, quintessentially human, but only because it is ultimately divine.

Paul's emphasis on love serves to highlight its place in the relationship between members of a community and between the community and God. Simply put, without love there can be no community, and without community there can be no shared hope and no shared faith. Love is the glue that keeps the community together, drawing upon each other's strengths. It is love that draws believers to God, because in God believers see the answer to their hope and, consequently, freedom from the suffering that keeps them bound.

Notice, though, that nowhere in Paul's description does he mention emotions or feelings. The biggest mistake people make is to equate love with feeling. We assume that love is something that (poof!) just happens when we see someone attractive. We "fall in love," as if love were some kind of accident that we can't help. It exerts some mysterious control over us, until (poof again!) we fall out of love and move on to the next "love" interest. Is this what Paul is talking about? Is this what Jesus teaches? Does this mean God "falls in love" with us, and can just as easily fall out of love with us?

Here is perhaps the best example of how our way of thinking and our language come up short. We just don't have a good grasp of what "love," in Paul's sense, really means. Part of the reason is that Paul was able to distinguish *love* from what we might otherwise call romance, friendship, sexual attraction, desire, passion, or something else. The Greeks had several words that all translate into the English word *love*. They had a more complex, more nuanced understanding of the depth of what love involves between human beings, not to mention between God and human beings. So when Paul wrote of love, he used the term *agape*, which may be roughly described as "self-giving love," to the point where it becomes sacrificial. When Jesus commands his disciples to "love one another . . . [j]ust as I have loved you" (John 13:34), he certainly is not saying "Feel passion for each other" or "Be friendly with each other." He says that our actions are to be self-giving in the way that Jesus is self-giving. Similarly, Jesus says, "Those who love me will keep my word, and my Father will love them, and we will come to them and make our home with them" (John 14:23). Again, he is not summoning people to *feel* a certain way, but to *live* a certain way, namely, following the commandments of Jesus (love God and neighbor) so that people may know the way God gives himself to people. Why? Because God is the source of life itself, and to be loved by God is to be the recipient of the life that God freely offers us.

The byproducts of love are those emotions that people see, so it is no surprise that we mistake the emotion for the reality. When I choose to love my wife—even in a simple way like doing the laundry or fixing something—she will sometimes thank me by doing something we might call *romantic*, like giving me a hug or a foot massage. It's her way of expressing the way she feels valued as a person; the feeling comes from being cared for, even on mundane levels. The romance is a response to something. It's fun, it gives us pleasure, and it helps us to be happy with each other. Love is what gives rise to these romantic feelings, and the consequent actions that people recognize, especially demonstrated on Valentine's Day. But a long-term relationship cannot be based solely on these emotions or expressions of love, unless they are based on the deeper reality of love.

When poets and novelists write about "falling in love," the key idea is not love per se, but rather the adrenaline-boosting *hope* for love. When someone "falls" for another, there is attraction: I want to be with you; I want you to be with me. But this is hope, not love. To be more precise: it is love that I am hoping for with you, and this hope gives rise to my emotions of desire and happiness. Further, this hope impels me to undertake the actions that I believe will help you "fall in love" with me: I present myself to you as one who will make you happy. I encourage you to see me as I see you, as a source of hope for love. I want you to feel like I do, and thus to want me the way I want you.

We fasten on the romantic idea of love because it represents the easiest, most delightful form of love, that which involves our explicit choice to be for another. It is easy to love one we have chosen as the recipient of love, because we are attracted to that person. We want to be for that person, because in doing so we experience a kind of self-transcendence, a going-out-of-self because the other makes us happy. But romance is a match, whereas love itself is a slow-burning fire. Unless the match becomes part of the fire, it burns out quickly. Romantic love expires if it is not supported by real love. Thus, romance must be allied with genuine love, which "bears all things, believes all things, hopes all things, endures all things." In other words, love must survive those times when it does not produce positive feelings.

The reason it is so tragic that many equate love and feeling is that feelings change, sometimes without our control. For this reason, many consider love fickle. But love transcends feelings when it becomes something we choose to do, a way we choose to live. We can choose to love even when it is painful and difficult. In a romantic relationship, there will be times of disillusionment, pain, withdrawal, lack of communication—but love enables us to get beyond these moments. Moreover, because we continue to love through these difficult times, the relationship actually thrives and continually gives rise to the positive feelings that characterize romance. The match is kept burning if it is part of the slow-burning fire.

If we can choose to love another when it does not produce good feelings for us, then it makes sense that we can choose to love even those we do not like. As noted earlier, one of the most difficult commandments of Jesus is "Love your enemies and pray for those who persecute you" (Matthew 5:44). This command is possible only if love and emotion are distinct—in other words, we can love an enemy only if we can love others without liking them. We can choose to pray for others, talk to others, even help others in spite of what they have done. The ill feelings may never leave; others may never say thanks or recognize our kindness. Why, then, love the enemy? Not necessarily for the enemy's sake, but for our own. The commandments of love are not utopian—Jesus is not trying to create some fiction where everyone gets along. Instead, he teaches that the act of love is what gives life to a human being. It is through loving others that we grow more and more into the image of God. We become better, wiser, more holy persons by practicing the commandments of love, especially in difficult circumstances. The harder it is to love a person, the greater the challenge, and the greater the reward.

> [Jesus said,] "For if you love those who love you, what reward to you have? Do not even the tax-collectors do the same? And if you greet only your brothers and sisters, what more are you doing than others? Do not even the Gentiles do the same? Be perfect, therefore, as your heavenly Father is perfect." (Matthew 5:46–48)

This call to perfection is not an unrealistic demand that we immediately overcome all our limitations, but rather an emphasis on the fact that we are called to be like God in the way that we love. To be human, Jesus seems to be saying, is to be uniquely qualified to act in the same way that God acts, to make of ourselves perfect persons; and the way to do this is to love in exactly the same way that God loves.

Love, then, becomes a kind of discipline. The commitment of faith is a radical assent to love God, which gives rise to the hope that this new faith is worthwhile. But the living of faith is love—in other words, in assenting to faith we assent to love God by loving the people we encounter, both when it is easy and, perhaps more importantly, when it is difficult. The discipline becomes important especially in those times when we are called to love in ways that aren't easy. Love sometimes demands that we undertake unpleasant tasks, and without faith and the hope that, in the end, they are of value, chances are we might avoid them.

Again, like the athlete who must undertake wearisome and sometimes dismal tasks in order to pursue her hope, Christians are called to love in ways that can be daunting. In our own lives, we encounter such experiences: reconciling with someone who has hurt us, sacrificing fun for someone who needs us now, taking on extra work in the belief that it will help others. In the larger scope of Christian love, there are stories of people who have devoted their life's work to feeding the poor, ministering to the leprous, working with AIDS patients, reading stories to children with cancer, teaching people new farming techniques in areas ravaged by famine, comforting destitute people who are dying in the streets, working with abused wives, gathering clothing for homeless people, and many more. To love is to seek not our own pleasure for the moment, but rather to seek goodness in the long haul—the kind of goodness that reaches into the depths of the soul, where we most earnestly yearn to love and be loved. We seek out the needy and love them because it is easy to do so, and it feeds the soul. Needy people often accept love readily and love readily in return, even if they cannot express it.

We are all needy, of course, but some of us are better at hiding it under the weight of careers, good health, pleasure, friends, money, entertainment, and all the other elements that make up postmodern culture. We hide our need because when we face it, we suffer. To be in need is to be in a position of dependence, and thus to recognize that we are incapable of completely fulfilling our own needs. But real love involves the exposure of our soul, and so in loving another we are at the same time exposing our own need to be loved. Many of us avoid love for this reason, because it can be initially frightening. We venture forth timidly, allowing ourselves to feel some of the things that go along with real love, especially the more positive feelings like sexual desire and thrill and happiness, but fail to go any deeper. To love another person is to donate our soul, and many think that in doing so they lose themselves.

The paradox, however, is that love is self-perpetuating: in donating ourselves, we learn that we have more to give. This is why we come to know ourselves most deeply through the practice, the discipline of love. In loving another, we discover the deepest parts of ourselves; and the more we love, the more we love in different ways, the more we discover our own souls.

God calls us to love because in the discipline of love, we discover that at the core of our souls is the love of God, constantly feeding our desire to love and be loved. Love is the "living water" that derives from the source, God, and which is channeled through the person choosing to love others.

> The LORD will guide you continually,
>   and satisfy your needs in parched places . . .
> and you shall be like a watered garden,
>   like a spring of water,
>   whose waters never fail (Isaiah 58:11).

> . . .

> [Jesus said,] ". . . but those who drink of the water that I will give them will never be thirsty. The water that I will give will become in them a spring of water gushing up to eternal life." (John 4:14)

The practice of love enables us to know that the Holy Spirit dwells within the depths of our souls, nourishing us and enabling us to be who we are. Love is the ultimate Christian virtue because it is the very fulfillment of faith and our desire for hope.

It is no surprise, then, that Christians, over their history, have developed an approach to living, an ethics that seeks to understand what love demands in everyday life. Think of the Ten Commandments: these are ethical principles that God gave to Moses as specific guidelines for how to love. Love demands honoring God, avoiding idols, keeping the Sabbath, honoring our parents, and avoiding acts that harm the community: killing, stealing, lying, adultery, and malicious jealousy for what other people have. These are general principles, though, and so

Christians of every age seek to understand further what love entails, both to honor God and to build up the community of the Church.

At the heart of Christian ethics, like any other system of ethics, is the understanding that people construct their lives around the choices they make. In effect, we create ourselves through what we do. So it is important to make sure that we make ourselves into good people. And in order to do this, we must make sure that our choices in life are good choices, especially when they are difficult ones.

In philosophy, the word often used to describe the study of ethics is *axiology*, the root of which gives us the word "axis." Everyone has an axis around which their lives turn—a basic philosophy of life that guides their choices and forms who they see themselves to be. We develop our axis throughout our lives. Young children, for example, are often guided by the axis "be a good boy/girl, and listen to Mom or Dad." Good and bad are simply a matter of obeying: I'm good when I obey, bad when I don't. Later on, though, as teenagers, these same people develop a different axis; then, as adults, they develop yet another axis, and so on throughout their lives. Some examples of different axes: "have fun," "get rich," "be popular," "create art," or "experience all of life." Sometimes people are very aware of the axis that guides their life choices, but at other times, they are unaware and feel that they have no basis for making good decisions. It is the burden of every person to understand what guides him or her through life.

The difficult point about axiology is the recognition that not all people choose a good axis. Those who live by the implicit principle "seek pleasure, avoid pain" eventually find themselves unable to enjoy anything. Other axes can be similarly limiting. So perhaps the ultimate challenge for human beings is to identify that axis which can guide them through the entirety of their lives, giving them a solid basis for all their life choices. Such an axis will be one that can adapt to the different stages of life, enable people to find healing when they choose wrong, give life to them at all times.

Christians believe that Jesus' commandments of love comprise such an axis. The simple formula "love God, love neighbor" is an axis that can guide our decisions throughout life, because it is the axis that is rooted in the very reality of who we are. Since the human being is created out of love by God, in order to love God freely, love is the very axis of our creation; and thus it is through the constant practice of love that we realize our full natures.

> [Jesus said,] "Everyone then who hears these words of mine and acts on them will be like a wise man who built his house on rock. The rain fell, the floods came, and the winds blew and beat on that house, but it did not fall, because it had been founded on rock." (Matthew 7:24–25)

There are many people in our culture who seem to go through life without much direction, swayed by every new thing that comes along. Others are so driven, either by greed or desire for fame or power, that they ignore other aspects of life. Still others come to that point in their lives when they question everything they had previously known, undergoing a crisis because they no longer know what to believe. There are many who, in the words of Thoreau, live "lives of quiet desperation" for want of something to give their lives meaning. These words of Jesus suggest that faith is the axis around which we can make loving choices, confident that our choices are secure, like rock. While we cannot be certain that our lives will be carefree, still we can know that love is lasting, and that through the practice of love, we can make ourselves into persons who are deeply good.

From Christian ethics we have inherited the understanding that every human being has a conscience that enables him or her to know what is good, because it is through the exercise of conscience that we come to know the goodness of God. Unfortunately, many people think of the conscience as that which prevents them from doing anything fun. Perhaps you can recall those commercials that show someone with an angel on one shoulder and a devil on the other, where the devil is the one telling the person to "just do it," referring to whatever seems more exciting. Further, we tend to think of conscience as a series of "thou shalt nots"—eat chocolate, drive fast, have sex, get drunk, whatever. But the conscience is much more than a tyrannical voice forbidding pleasure. Rather, the conscience is our deepest self, that which reminds us of our axis and helps us understand how to choose those things that make us the person we really want to be. While it is true that there are some "thou shalt nots" in Christian theology, they exist simply because there are some actions that can never be loving. What is important, though, is to remember that real love sometimes requires difficult choices, and we are blessed to have a part of us that reminds us of that fact regularly.

Like any other part of us, though, conscience must be exercised or it will fail us. Clearly, there are those who do not exercise conscience—there are evil people in the world. But many of us are just lazy, choosing to ignore what we know is right and, instead, choosing what is convenient or nonthreatening. In doing so, we act against our real selves. Sin is not some abstract concept, some scorecard on which God records the times we disobey. This is a childish notion. Rather, sin is the choice to act against conscience, and therefore to act against the persons we have chosen for ourselves to be. It is a choice against love and against God, who wishes our goodness even more than we do. Fortunately, regardless of how often we exercise our conscience, God loves us anyway and constantly seeks our attention, even when we ignore God.

If true wisdom involves knowing and doing good, then conscience is what gives us wisdom. But conscience itself can do nothing unless it is nourished by that which gives it life. In other words, we can't expect to do good unless we learn and practice choosing good when it is difficult to do so. Love is the discipline of choosing good in everything we do, so that our desire to do good grows with our ability. Those who love in the small matters are more able to love in greater ones, even to the point of self-sacrifice. This, too, is a paradox of love, that in giving ourselves away we find ourselves.

The greatest difficulty of love, though, is not the idea of love but the reality of loving right now, in this moment. Anyone can aspire to be a loving person, great in the sight of others and chosen as a daughter or son of God. But to genuinely love someone is to act in silence, often unnoticed and unappreciated, sometimes doing that which is unpleasant. Love is less often public heroism than private perseverance. Love is cleaning up after others, taking out the trash, pausing in our busy day to do something we weren't asked to do but nevertheless needs to be done. Love is giving way to a person merging into the busy highway, listening to a less than interesting story, going out of our way to greet a surly neighbor. Love is the courage to do what is right even if everyone thinks we're crazy. Love is honoring the request of a beloved, even if the request doesn't make sense. Love is admitting we're wrong.

The one who practices love becomes good at it. Once we become lovers, in the words of Kierkegaard, "the world—no matter how imperfect—becomes rich and beautiful, for it consists solely of opportunities for love." When we love, life takes on new meaning, for we see it no longer as a place where we must fight for survival, but rather as a place where we can practice loving and thereby practice wisdom. We begin to see beyond the evil things that people do, recognizing their woundedness and their inability to act freely. We become able to love even those others cannot love, for we understand the ways that they have become isolated, angry, and afraid. We choose to see each person as God intended him or her, or at least to try, and thus to free ourselves from the control of other people's actions. Instead of responding to anger with our own anger, we try to understand how others' negative actions give us new chances to love. We are fully free, because we choose to live not in reaction to what others do to us, but in constant vigilance for opportunities to love as we choose. And all this is possible because through our faith, we have the constant hope that our loving behavior will not only make us better people, but, in the end, will help us stand before God and testify with certainty, "Because you have loved me, I choose now to love you in return."

> Nothing is more practical than finding God, that is, than falling in love in a quite absolute, final way. What seizes your imagination, will affect everything. It will decide what will get you out of bed in the morning, what you do with your evenings, how you spend your weekends, what you read, who you know, what breaks your heart, and what amazes you with joy and gratitude. Fall in love, stay in love, and it will decide everything (Pedro Arrupe, S.J.).

For Group Discussion

1. What do you think faith is? What have you learned about faith, either in religious education or through experience? Where do you see examples of faith in action? How does this understanding of faith compare to what you see among ordinary Christians, for example, in your church?
2. What story, from the Bible or elsewhere, teaches you about faith?
3. What do you hope for, in the short run and long run? How do your life choices reflect what you hope for?
4. What experiences in your life have made it difficult for you to hope?
5. Consider one of the communities you belong to. What are the hopes of the community? How does it pursue those hopes? What are some of the disagreements people have within that community?
6. What has been your most profound experience of being loved? Of loving?
7. What factors in your life make it difficult for you to love?
8. What is your ethical axis? (Think realistically!)

The Banquet of Wisdom: We Can Choose to Respond to the Invitation

Christian spirituality is a tradition of wisdom we can draw on to address our most fundamental needs as human beings. It is difficult, however, to approach this tradition without "baggage," good or bad, because we live in a society that has been influenced in many ways by this tradition. However, society today is no longer explicitly Christian in ways that past generations were—especially those in Western Europe from which millions of Americans migrated, and which gave to American society the language and ideologies that still influence us today.

Historian of religion Catherine Albanese has distinguished "ordinary religion," which she writes is more or less the same as culture, from "extraordinary religion," which is more about our encounter with the sacred. Twenty-first-century America is, in some ways, moving beyond the ordinary religion that characterized the dominant ethos in this country from the time of the founding fathers through the twentieth century. This ordinary religion was a form of Christianity; simple evidence like the structure of holidays and working patterns tell us that most Americans thought that Christianity and ordinary living went hand in hand. Today, however, our society is much more pluralistic, and with growing numbers of faithful Muslims, Jews, Buddhists, Hindus, Taoists, and others, it is less useful to think of American society as practicing the ordinary religion of Christianity. Thus, we are confronted with a sea of options for practicing our spirituality, and Christianity is only one of them. I offer this book as a way of entering into the practices and thinking of Christian tradition, even for those who have these other options.

German theologian Karl Rahner remarked that the Christian of the future will be a mystic, or will not *be*. Because we are shedding our ordinary religion, those whose practice of Christianity was based on cultural conditions are finding less and less reason to maintain the same practices. The positive side of this, though, is that we are challenged to ask basic questions of faith: Why practice at all? Fortunately, such questions lead people to more seriously consider Christian spirituality as the source of faithful practice. We no longer have to go to church simply because everyone else is doing it; rather, we must choose to go to church because we believe it is the place where we want to respond to God's invitation. The complexities and diversities of today's world move us to consider Christianity as extraordinary religion, a tradition that invites us into a deeper and deeper contemplation of divine mysteries.

Christian spirituality is of great value to young people like me living in this postmodern, pluralistic society. Far from enclosing us in an arcane world, insulated from the rest of society, Christianity today opens us to consider more carefully the world we live in. It challenges us to develop a new vision, one that we can call sacramental, which enables us to see in all people and things the fingerprint of a mysterious God. For too long Christians have assumed that young people would absorb what it means to be Christian simply by living in a Christian society, and that this pattern would continue. In my experience both as a professor and as a religious educator, this is no longer the case. Gen2K has grown up in a diverse society, and many have learned only ordinary religion. Many have not been given the opportunity to see Christianity as offering us an encounter with the sacred, with meaning, with God. If you are one of these people, then I offer this suggestion: don't let your baggage keep you from embarking on a spiritual journey. Christian spirituality is a banquet of wisdom, but if you think that all the food is out of date, you may not be able to taste its rich substance. Challenge those ideas and discover for yourself. Ultimately, the only test of whether or not food is good is to sit down and eat.

Suggested Biblical Texts for Prayer

(Especially for newcomers)[1]

Below are listed biblical texts, with suggestions on how to use them in prayer. You will need a copy of a Bible for these suggestions to be useful; I recommend a contemporary translation rather than an older version, for the simple reason that it will be easier to understand. If you are unfamiliar with reading the Bible, most versions have a table of contents and explanations on how to find the various books.

There is no particular order to these suggestions; you may choose to do them in order or to pick one that seems to suit you at the moment. It can be useful to pray the same text more than once, paying attention to the changes you sense from the last time you prayed.

Free yourself of expectations in prayer; treat it as you would any new activity, where some things will go wrong. Pay attention to what thoughts, feelings, images, and ideas come into your mind as you pray; observe them without judging to learn what they tell you.

Initially, spend just a few minutes in prayer; don't set lofty goals. As you progress, you may find yourself wanting to spend more time. Find a place where there aren't distractions; make yourself comfortable; relax. Imagine you are just hanging out with your best friend. It's not far from the truth. As you read, try to imagine you and God having a conversation, each listening to the other. What does the way you imagine God speaking tell you about your image of God? You might want to begin using a prayer journal as a place to reflect on your experiences in prayer, so you can revisit them later. Finally, I suggest you try to find a community that can help you: a church, a prayer group, or a peer discussion group.

Who Am I?

1. Psalm 139:1–18 (God knows me)
Read the psalm slowly and deliberately. Imagine that you are talking directly to God using the words of the psalm. Pay attention to what you feel as you read: thankfulness? resentment? confusion? Do not dwell on any of these feelings, but simply acknowledge them. Then think about them after you are finished reading. What does the presence of these feelings tell you about God and the way you view God? Speak to God about these feelings. Listen.

2. Luke 18:9–14 (the Pharisee and the tax collector)
Imagine yourself in the story that Jesus tells. What do you see, hear, smell, feel? Which character do you identify with more? Imagine yourself as the tax collector. Why have you come to the Temple? What are your feelings? What do you do when you leave the Temple? How do Jesus' observations about you change the way you feel?

3. Philippians 3:7–16 (Christ as my goal)
What would it be like for you to give up everything for Christ? How would your life be different? What do you think God is calling you to do with your particular talents and gifts? What are your life goals? Do you think God is calling you to these goals? Ask God to help you understand what your goals should be, and ask for God's help in achieving them.

Who Is God?

1. 1 John 4:7–11 (God is love)
What does this text tell you about spirituality? What is an example from your own life when you felt loved? Can you picture God being the one who was loving you through that person? Can you picture God being the one who gives you the ability to love someone else? Ask God how to love. Listen.

2. Luke 15:11–32 (the generous father)

Put yourself into the story, first as the son, then as the father. What do you feel? see? hear? smell? As the son, what is it like to go back to the father? As the father, what is it like to welcome the son? Pay attention to your feelings as you imagine yourself in the story. What do your feelings tell you about who God is? Speak to God about your feelings, then listen.

3. Psalm 23 (the shepherd)

Dwell on each image that this song presents. Which image strikes you? Why does the writer use the image of the shepherd? Imagine you were speaking this psalm to God directly. How would you feel? Speak to God, and listen.

Who Is Jesus?

1. Philippians 2:6–11 (the hymn about Jesus)

What words strike you in this prayer? Imagine you are speaking to Jesus and asking him about what is written in this hymn. What do you say to him? What does he say in response?

2. John 3:16–17 (God's only son)

What does this reading tell you about God? about Jesus? about the way Jesus went about his life? Why did Jesus come as such a seemingly insignificant person, rather than, for example, a political leader? Imagine asking Jesus these questions. How does he respond?

3. John 2:1–11 (the wedding at Cana)

Why did Jesus change the water into wine? What does this tell you about him? Imagine yourself in the story: as the bridegroom, as the waiter, as Mary, as Jesus. What are your impressions? Again, apply your senses to your imagination of the story. Pay attention to your feelings, then speak to Jesus about them. What do you want to ask Jesus? What does he say in reply?

What Should I Do?

1. Luke 5:1–11 (the call of the disciples)
Can you identify with the fishermen? Have you had an experience of trying hard to do something, then giving up in frustration? Imagine Jesus coming to you in that situation. What would he have said? What would you have said to him? Would your response have been like Simon Peter's? Speak to Jesus about this. What does he say to you?

2. John 15:9–13 (love one another)
How has Jesus loved you? Have there been people in your life who show you love the way Jesus loved? In what ways can you love people you encounter in your everyday life? Ask Jesus to help you to know how to do this. What does he say?

3. Matthew 19:16–22 (seeking perfection)
What is your reaction to Jesus' answer to the rich young man? Why does Jesus refer to money? Do any of your possessions keep you from following Jesus as you would want? Ask Jesus how he wants you to follow him. What does he say? How do you feel about it? What does it tell you about your priorities?

Prologue

1. The term *Generation X* has sometimes been used in a critical sense
   to refer to the "slackers" whose values are not the same as those of
   Baby Boomers. The very use of the "X" can be seen as a "lack of something," and so perhaps is not the best term to use of an entire cohort
   of young adults. Similarly, then, the term *Generation Y* often means
   "younger Generation X," and thus suffers from the same problem.
   Another term that has recently found currency is the generation of
   millenials—this term is closer to what I am trying to suggest, namely
   that the experience of being young during the passing of the new millennium will have a formative impact on many people.

2. For an overview of several studies of Catholics, see Dean R. Hoge
   et al., *Young Adult Catholics: Religion in the Culture of Choice* (Notre
   Dame, IN: University of Notre Dame Press, 2001), pp. 16–18. In
   their survey, 80 percent of respondents indicated that they consider
   themselves spiritual persons (see p. 154), but there is a lower level
   of Mass attendance compared to thirty years ago (see p. 160). In
   summarizing their findings, the authors write, "Research on religion today points to the uncoupling of religion from spirituality, to
   organized religion's waning monopoly over the sacred, and to spiritual seeking outside the parameters of institutional religion."

Chapter One

1. "B.C.E" stands for "before the common era," and is used by more and
   more people rather than the older term "B.C." or "before Christ."

Similarly, the term "C.E." ("common era") is used in place of the older "A.D." (*Anno Domini*, Latin for "in the year of the Lord").

Chapter Two

1. Saint Teresa of Avila suggested that in seeking *arrobamiento* (spiritual ecstasy), many people actually practice *abobamiento* (foolishness).

Chapter Three

1. The following seven books are *deuterocanonical*, meaning they are found only in Catholic and Orthodox Bibles: Tobit, Judith, Wisdom, Sirach (Ecclesiasticus), Baruch, 1 and 2 Maccabees. In addition, there are certain additions to Esther and Daniel that are not found in Protestant Bibles. Certain Orthodox Bibles contain 3 and 4 Maccabees, 1 and 2 Esdras, the Prayer of Manasseh, and Psalm 151. For a more complete history of the Bible, see James R. Beasley et al., *An Introduction to the Bible* (Nashville: Abingdon Press, 1991); Lawrence Boadt, *Reading the Old Testament: An Introduction* (New York/Mahwah, NJ: Paulist Press, 1984); Pheme Perkins, *Reading the New Testament* (New York/Mahwah, NJ: Paulist Press, 1988).

Chapter Four

1. Alasdair Macintyre, *After Virtue* (Notre Dame, IN: University of Notre Dame Press, 1984).
2. C. S. Lewis uses the term *mere Christianity* in his book of the same title, to suggest this idea of what is common to all who believe in Jesus.
3. This criticism is a sign of hope, for it expresses the desire that the Church be meaningful. To desire that an organization change is to desire that it become more welcoming to people like me. It may represent the manifestation of a young person's wish to have a better understanding of faith.
4. For this point, I am indebted to Dr. Luke Timothy Johnson, Candler Professor of New Testament and Christian Origins, Emory University.

5. Fyodor Dostoyevsky, *The Brothers Karamazov.* Translated by Constance Garnett (New York: The Modern Library), pp. 55 and 57.

6. For a summary of some of these studies, see "Revenge of the Church Ladies," in *USA Today,* February 11, 1999, p. 15A, which cites several university studies that suggest religious couples are the most sexually satisfied.

7. "Wonder, Eroticism, and Enigma," in James B. Nelson and Sandra P. Longfellow, eds., *Sexuality and the Sacred* (Louisville: John Knox Press, 1994), pp. 80–84.

Appendix

1. There are many good books available to help people develop a prayer life. One series, which is beneficial for both newcomers and people who are used to praying, either alone or in groups, is Mark Link, S.J., *Vision 2000: Praying Scripture in a Contemporary Way* (Allen, TX: Tabor Publishing, 1992).